Assessment First

Deborah White

SCHOLASTIC

New York • Toronto • London • Auckland • Sydney
Mexico City • New Delhi • Hong Kong • Buenos Aires

Acknowledgments

Tennyson said, "I am a part of all I've met." I've been lucky in my professional life to have the opportunity to take on parts of so many people: Marie Clay, Ellin Keene, Linda Hoyt, Debbie Miller, Patricia Cunningham, Richard Allington, David Pearson. The list could go on and on. Some I've met only through their writing. Some I've had the pleasure to meet face to face. Although most of these people don't even know me, they have made me into who I am professionally. To all the experts who have shaped my beliefs about teaching reading, thank you.

I could never have dreamed to take on this project without the encouragement of my truly exceptional editor, Sarah Longhi, who made me believe that maybe it really was possible, and my wonderful colleague at the Bureau of Education and Research, Jeannie Donoghue. Thank you both for your belief in me. Thank you to Christy Perry, who got this whole merry-go-round spinning with that "little application" for me to fill out.

Thanks to my friend and traveling partner Karen Anderson, who patiently listened to and encouraged me.

Thank you to the students at Lyle Elementary School, who taught me so much about how children become readers.

Thank you especially to my family, Wade, Travis, and Nathan, who supported and encouraged me and put up with undone chores and busy weekends while I sat at the computer. Yours are the best parts of me.

Finally, to the reader, I hope a little of me becomes a part of you.

Credits

Pages 11 and 159: Informal Reading Inventory forms reprinted from *Classroom Reading Inventory*, 9th Ed. (McGraw Hill) © copyright 2001 by Silvaroli, N. and Wheelock, W.

Page 133: Oral Reading Fluency Scale adapted by T. V. Rasinski © copyright 2004 in *Assessing Reading Fluency*, Pacific Resources for Education and Learning Honolulu, HI. Original rubric from *Listening to Children Read Aloud: Oral Fluency* by G. S. Pinnell, J. J. Pikulski, K. K. Wixson, J. R. Campbell, P. B. Gough, & A. S. Beatty, 1995, Washington, D. C.: U.S. Department of Education, National Center for education Statistics.

Page 134: Multidimensional Fluency Rubric adapted by T. V. Rasinski © copyright 2004 in *Assessing Reading Fluency*, Pacific Resources for Education and Learning Honolulu, HI. Original rubric from "Training Teachers to Attend to Their Students' Oral Reading Fluency" by J. Zutell and T. V. Rasinski, 1991, *Theory Into Practice*, 30, pp. 211–217.

Page 145: Selection from *You Can't Eat Your Chicken Pox, Amber Brown* (Putnam) © copyright 1995 by Paula Danzinger.

Page 184: Page from *What a Day* (Shortland, Ltd) © copyright 1987 by Sally Farrell Odgers (text) and by Mary Davy (illustrations).

Page 185: Page from *The Fox Who Foxed* (Rigby) © copyright 1987 by Beverley Milburn (text) and by Nelson Price Milburn (illustrations).

Edited by Sarah Longhi
Copyedited by David Klein
Cover design by Jason Robinson
Cover photos (clockwise from top): © Anderson Ross/Getty Images;
© Michael Newman/PhotoEdit; Blend Images/Punchstock
Interior design by Kelli Thompson

ISBN-13: 978-0-545-02122-7
ISBN-10: 0-545-02122-7

Copyright © 2008 by Deborah White.
All rights reserved. Published by Scholastic Inc.
Printed in the U.S.A.

1 2 3 4 5 6 7 8 9 10   40   15 14 13 12 11 10 09 08

Contents

Foreword

Assessment First is truly an appropriate name for this book. Effective instruction always begins with knowledge of the students being taught. Knowing students' current levels of performance in reading as well as their strengths and concerns is essential to developing instruction that corresponds to students' needs. This is assessment as its best. Once we know where students are in reading, we also need to know if the instruction we provide is having the desired outcome. If not, we need to alter that instruction. Monitoring students' progress in reading is also an important part of assessment. Assessment that is formative, that leads to effective instruction for students, is not only a good first step, it also must be ongoing.

At Kent State University I teach a course in the diagnosis and remediation of reading difficulties. I also direct our university's summer reading clinic for struggling readers. In both of these activities, assessment is crucial. When working with struggling readers we need to know more than the level of students' performance. We also need to diagnose the cause of their reading problems as well as determine their strengths and interests. Once this assessment work is done, instruction can be designed to meet those needs, drawing on the strengths and interests that the students possess. From the information we gain through the diagnosis and assessment of students, we design instruction that has the best chance of being successful. And indeed, our work with struggling readers in the KSU reading clinic has been, without question, effective.

This approach to effective instruction—instruction that comes from a thorough understanding of individual readers—is the same approach that Deborah White takes in this volume. Not only does she begin with the premise that assessment and diagnosis of reading problems drives instruction, but she focuses her assessment on the key competencies of reading that all students must master in order to develop full proficiency in literacy: phonemic awareness, phonics or word decoding, reading fluency, vocabulary, and comprehension. These reading competencies have been validated by empirical research and reported by the National Reading Panel (2000).

Deborah White's approach to assessment in reading is theoretically sound, empirically validated, and reasonable and practical to teachers and reading specialists who work in the trenches with students on a daily basis. In addition to a format that should make sense to any teacher who reads the book, I applaud Deborah's informal, teacher-centered approach to assessment. Deborah recognizes that the teacher is the best person to make sense of a student's reading skills and needs. Rather than rely solely on formal tests of reading that provide a standard and percentile score and a grade equivalent on some generalize measure of reading achievement, Deborah makes it perfectly clear that only an informed and observant teacher can make the fine-grained assessments of students' reading that can lead to effective instruction. With *Assessment First*, she honors every teacher who has ever thoughtfully and carefully tried to understand readers and reading.

Deborah's book moves the field of reading assessment and instruction forward. I urge you to read through this well written text twice—first to get the general sense of Deborah's thoughtful approach to assessment, and a second time to examine the specific details that she provides in making effective assessment work for you and your students. It's about time that our profession recognizes that literacy instruction can be effective only when literacy assessment comes first.

Timothy Rasinski, Ph.D.
Professor of Education
Reading and Writing Center
Kent State University

Reference

National Reading Panel. (2000). *Report of the National Reading Panel: Teaching children to read. Report of the subgroups*. Washington, DC: U.S. Department of Health and Human Services, National Institutes of Health.

Introduction

More assessment? Are you kidding? Doesn't it already seem that we spend way too much time assessing our students? What about some time for teaching?

I've been a reading specialist for the last 14 years, and I've given my share of assessments, including benchmark tests, informal reading inventories, fluency tests, and state-mandated reading tests. Many of those tests collected information for someone else to use, not me. The assessments evaluated my program, my curriculum, my school, and even my district. Sometimes results of the assessments arrived in a timely manner, but other times my students had moved on to another grade or school before I ever saw the scores. Many of the tests told me only one thing: My students were struggling with reading. Whatever the test was measuring, my students weren't measuring up. But the scores on the tests didn't tell me how to help my students. They didn't always tell me what the students *could* do. And most important, the scores didn't tell me what to do next.

I've designed this book for a different kind of assessment approach. This book will help you make instructional planning decisions based on the results of a variety of reading assessments you can use with your students. The assessments cover the range of reading components identified by the

Each chapter provides you with the following:

- Samples of completed assessments and a thorough analysis with plans for what to do next

- Steps and forms for giving the assessments

- Charts and tools for organizing information about your students and setting up flexible, targeted instruction groups

- A bank of appropriate teaching activities and techniques to use, based on your findings

- References and suggestions for further reading

Report of the National Reading Panel in 2000: phonemic awareness and phonics, vocabulary, fluency, and comprehension, plus how to find your students' instructional levels. But unlike other assessments you may have used, these assessments will give you immediate, useful information about your students so you can plan your instructional focus and activities to move your students along the path toward becoming capable, independent readers. Using the assessments first will help you decide what to teach tomorrow.

So how do you get started? Chapter 1 begins by showing you how to gather three levels of information about your students by listening to them read. First you'll **determine an appropriate instructional level for your students**. Next, by watching what they do and paying attention to the kinds of errors they make, you'll **determine what information from the text is helping them the most in their reading**. Finally, you will **understand which helpful reading strategies your students already have in place**. Then you are ready to plan instruction to meet the needs of your students. Chapter 1 also includes suggestions for which of the other chapters will be most useful for further assessments you will want to use, based on the information you collect from your first tests.

Do you have students who struggle to read words accurately? Are you unsure of their ability to use letters and sounds? Chapter 2 covers both **phonemic awareness** and **phonics**, the essential components for reading at the word level. Here are assessment techniques to determine your students' strengths and weaknesses with hearing and effectively using sound-symbol relationships, from kindergarten up through reading multisyllabic words in the intermediate grades. Follow-up activities and techniques such as Be the Sentence and Break It Apart help you target the specific word skills students need to practice.

Sometimes students have strong phonics skills, but still struggle with understanding the meanings of words, or recognizing high-frequency words that don't fit common phonics patterns. Chapter 3 covers **vocabulary**, including sight words. This important and often neglected area contributes to both reading comprehension and fluency. The tools in this chapter allow you to gather information about your students' existing knowledge of words, as well as their ability to use word-learning strategies such as context clues and word parts to understand unfamiliar words. Activities such as Make-a-Word and Picture This enable you to effectively teach not only your own selected vocabulary, but these important strategies as well.

Many of my students read text accurately, but with so many breaks in fluency or so slowly that they can't understand what they've read. Does this sound familiar? Chapter 4 covers this important area of **fluency** and includes tools to assess your students' reading fluency beyond simply the number of words read per minute. Since fluency has such an impact on comprehension, this chapter helps you to plan effective instruction for students who have difficulty with pace, expression, phrasing, and smoothness, and suggests specific teaching techniques and activities including "reading trains" to use for each of these important areas.

I have students (and you probably do, too) who read aloud with accuracy, fluency, and expression, and who give every indication that they are doing fine, but when we talk I find that they don't understand much of what they've read. Chapter 5 is the most important for these students, and for many others. It covers **comprehension**, the whole purpose for reading. This chapter includes effective ways to assess not only whether comprehension has occurred, but what comprehension strategies students are successfully using. You'll find lessons to teach students how to use eight different strategies, such as visualizing and using text structure, as they read to fully comprehend both fiction and expository text.

Every one of these chapters includes the most powerful methods I've found to gather useful information about students and their reading abilities. These assessments, planning tools, and suggested teaching activities and strategies will make a positive difference in your teaching and in your students' achievement. The time you spend getting to know your students with these assessments will enable you to use your remaining time with them for planning and teaching.

Maybe we do have time for some more assessments, after all.

Resources and Further Reading

National Reading Panel. (2000). *Report of the National Reading Panel: Teaching children to read. Report of the subgroups.* Washington, DC: U.S. Department of Health and Human Services, National Institutes of Health.

Chapter 1

Determining Students' Reading Levels and Your Instructional Focus

Classroom Snapshot

Mrs. Anderson calls a small group of her first-grade students to the reading table. As they gather, each student selects a book from a collection in the tub in the middle of the table. In quiet voices, the students begin reading, either alone or with a partner. Mrs. Anderson sits next to one of the children, and hands her the book the group read together yesterday. As Katie begins reading, Mrs. Anderson makes notes on a blank piece of paper, taking a running record of Katie's reading behaviors. When Katie finishes, teacher and child discuss the reading.

"That's a pretty funny story, isn't it? I really liked the part where they got Dad out of the bed, didn't you? You sure made his voice sound surprised when you read it," Mrs. Anderson comments. "Katie, I want to look at what you did on this page. I noticed when you read this part you stopped and went back. Do you remember why you did that?"

"It wasn't making sense right there so I reread the sentence. I saw I had a word wrong, so I changed it."

"That's right! You noticed that even though that word began with *un-*, it wasn't the word *under*, was it? It really helps to notice the endings of words, and check to see that what you are reading makes sense. I'd like you to take a look at this page right here. Will you reread this part? Make sure that you are checking that every word looks right at the end and makes sense, too."

Mrs. Anderson is using an informal assessment of Katie's reading to make decisions about her instruction. She is checking to see that her selected book is at Katie's instructional level and taking a look at the strategies Katie is using in order to decide what to teach next to encourage Katie's reading growth.

In this chapter we will discuss how running records and informal reading inventories will help you design your instruction for both individual students and groups. We'll look at ways to administer and score the assessments, and the kinds of information these assessments can give you, from a student's appropriate instructional reading level to the reading strategies that he or she uses most often when reading.

What happens inside a student's head while reading? So much of the processing and thinking that occur are invisible to us. How can we tell what strategies and information about text students are using when they read? The closest we can get to knowing how a student processes text is by making a record of the actual behaviors he or she exhibits while reading. Observing closely what the child says and does while reading can give us a window into the brain. While some of our assumptions are guesswork based on our observations, careful attention to such things as errors, pauses, rereading, and omissions can give us clues about the strategies our student is using. This information is most easily collected via a running record or informal reading inventory.

What Are Running Records and Informal Reading Assessments?

A running record is an assessment used to record, score, and analyze a child's reading behaviors while he is reading a text. Marie Clay's *An Observation Survey of Early Literacy Achievement* (1993) has a complete discussion of the running record. If you have more questions after reading this chapter, I highly recommend reading it. (See the resources at the end of this chapter.)

The running record is an integral component of Clay's Reading Recovery program. Trained teachers working individually with struggling first-grade readers use the information gathered from a daily running record on the book each child read the previous day to make teaching decisions. In the classroom setting, we can use running records to determine appropriate texts for individuals and groups, plan large- and small-group lessons, and conduct individual interventions for our students.

Running records are most easily used with beginning readers reading at a relatively slow rate, and they can be administered using any text. Teachers can record information about the students' reading on a blank piece of paper or on a copy of the text. It's an assessment you can do anywhere and anytime. I've even been known to dig a piece of paper out of the recycle bin to use for a running record when the opportunity to informally assess a student unexpectedly presents itself.

An Informal Reading Inventory (IRI), despite the name, is a slightly more formal assessment than a running record. It consists of leveled reading passages along with comprehension questions. It is more commonly used with older or more advanced readers who are reading at a faster rate, although it can be used with beginning readers as well. A number of commercial informal reading inventories are available, and basal reading series quite often have an inventory, such as the one shown at right, as part of their support materials. A little more preparation is required prior to using the IRI, as copies of the recording sheet must be made ahead of time. You can collect the same types of information from both running records and IRIs. Let's see what we might find out from running records and IRIs, and then how we give these assessments.

FORM A: Pretest   Part 2/Level 1 (71 Words)

Background Knowledge Assessment: This story is about puppies. What can you tell me about puppies?

Adequate [   ]   Inadequate [   ]

MARIA'S PUPPIES

Maria has two puppies.
She thinks that puppies are fun to watch.
The puppies' names are *Sissy* and *Sassy*.
Puppies are born with their eyes closed.
Their ears are closed, too.
This is why they use their smell and touch.
After two weeks, puppies begin to open their eyes and ears.
Most puppies can bark after four weeks.
Maria knows that *Sissy* and *Sassy* will grow up to be good pets.

Comprehension Check

(F) 1. _____ How many puppies does Maria have? (Two)

(F) 2. _____ What are the puppies' names? (Sissy and Sassy)

(I) 3. _____ Why do you think that Maria thinks puppies are fun to watch? (Any reasonable answer; e.g., they jump, roll around, chase their tails)

(F) 4. _____ What can puppies do after four weeks? (Bark)

(F) 5. _____ At birth, puppies must use their sense of smell and touch. Why? (Eyes or ears closed)

Scoring Guide   First

SIG WR Errors		COMP Errors	
IND	0	IND	0–1
INST	3	INST	1½–2
FRUST	6+	FRUST	2½+

Inventory Record for Teachers, FORM A: Pretest   57

An Informal Reading Inventory recording sheet for grade 1 from *Classroom Reading Inventory, Ninth Edition,* by Nicholas J. Silvaroli and Warren H. Wheelock, (McGraw Hill, 2001). Notice that the text has been printed out for you (students have their own copy of the passage) and there are questions to ask students to assess comprehension.

Like a running record, an IRI can be used in a variety of ways. First, you can establish a baseline for a student's reading level. If you use a leveled text for the assessment you can determine the grade or level at which a student can read and his or her percentage of accuracy. For example, if a student reads a second grade–level passage with 98 percent accuracy, we consider the text his independent level, while a student who reads the same text with only 88 percent accuracy is working at his frustration level. The second student may be able to read a first grade–level passage with 92 percent accuracy, which would indicate an instructional level of first grade. See the chart below for determining these reading levels.

Reading Accuracy	Text Level	Support
Below 90%	Hard or frustration level	Significant teacher support is required for the child to read the text successfully.
90%–94%	Instructional level	Some support is needed, for example, a guided-reading format.
95% and above	Easy or independent level	Little support is needed.

This information can be useful for determining initial instruction level, guided reading group placement, or intervention requirements. You can also use this information on report cards, or as a comparison for determining progress from the beginning to the end of the year.

There is more to find out about your students' reading abilities than simply their accuracy and appropriate reading level, however. At the second level of analysis, you can determine the kinds of information a student is using to read text. Is he or she using phonics, language structure, or, perhaps, memory of the text? Perhaps your student is focusing on pictures and what makes sense. Finding out what kinds of information the student is using right now to read will help you determine what kinds of instruction he or she needs next. This information is valuable for designing lessons and placing children in need-based groups. It also helps you determine what kinds of prompts and coaching statements will be most effective when reading with your students individually.

Numbers Note

These percentage guidelines were developed by Marie Clay as part of her Reading Recovery program and are a good starting place for assessing accuracy in reading. However, you may see other percentage ranges identified as independent, instruction, and frustration levels when using other materials, such as Beaver and Carter's *Developmental Reading Assessment* and other reading inventory sources. Whichever norms you use, keep in mind that it's much more important to analyze the types of errors a reader makes, rather than to rely on a single number.

At the third level of analysis, you can see the active strategies your student uses. Does he or she notice when there is a mistake or monitor the reading in other ways? Does your student have any strategies for word solving? What does he or she do when there is a difficulty? Having this information about students will help you determine what kinds of whole- and small-group strategy lessons you will design for your class.

We will look at all three levels of analysis. But first, let's learn the basic method of taking a running record or an IRI.

ADMINISTERING A RUNNING RECORD OR IRI

You administer a running record while sitting beside a child while he or she reads a text, usually one read only once before. (For establishing a baseline level, it should be a text he or she has never seen before.) Your role is to be an observer. Your job is to watch closely and record as much of the child's behavior while reading as possible. You should try very hard to remain neutral, not smiling and nodding as the child works through a text, or giving any indication as to whether he or she is correct. (This can be very difficult for teachers.) If the child gets totally stuck and cannot move on, you can tell the student a word. However, as we will see, you get very little information about a child when you do tell words. Avoid this as much as possible. Sometimes I literally have to put my hand over my mouth so I don't say anything to the child as he or she is reading. The whole idea of the running record is to see what a child can do without any assistance.

Procedure

1. As the child reads, record accurate reading on a running record form or blank sheet of paper with a check mark for each word. If what the child says differs from the text, record it by writing the substitution above the actual word. Here are some examples of how you would take a record of an accurate reading of "The Gingerbread Man," and a reading with a few errors.

Accurate reading of text	Record
"Run, run, as fast as you can,	✓ ✓ ✓ ✓ ✓ ✓
You can't catch me	✓ ✓ ✓ ✓
I'm the gingerbread man."	✓ ✓ ✓ ✓

What You Can Learn From an IRI

Level 1 A reader's accuracy rate (based on the number of errors he or she makes)

Level 2 The type of information the reader uses when he or she makes or corrects errors (meaning, language structure, and visual)

Level 3 The strategies a reader uses to read and understand a text

Inaccurate reading of text   **Record**

"Run, run, as fast as you can,   ✓ ✓ ✓ ✓ ✓ ✓

You won't catch me   ✓ won't ✓ ✓
                                            ‾‾‾‾‾
                                            can't

'cause I'm the gingerbread boy."   cause ✓ ✓ ✓ boy
                                         ‾‾‾‾‾   ‾‾‾
                                           —   man

The line underneath 'cause is there because the student inserted the word where there was no text. If the child left out *as*, record it this way:

Reading with omissions   **Record**

"Run, run, fast as you can,"   ✓ ✓ — ✓ ✓ ✓ ✓
                                            as

Put slashes in between sentences when there are multiple sentences on one line, like this:

Text with two sentences   **Record**

"I can run. I like to run."   ✓ ✓ ✓/✓ ✓ ✓ ✓

2. Try to record as much information about the reader's behavior as you can, so you will have some evidence to make guesses about what is going on in the child's head when reading. See the Running Record Coding Conventions chart on page 15 for a complete code for recording student behaviors.

If you are using an Informal Reading Inventory, the text each student has to read is printed out for you. You can use the same coding system by simply recording directly on the printed copy. Because students reading at higher levels often read more quickly, you can skip the checks for accurate reading and simply record substitutions, omissions, insertions, and the other behaviors. Otherwise it's difficult to keep up with the student's reading. Even so, I sometimes get a little behind if the child is making a lot of errors. It's okay to occasionally ask the child to stop and let you catch up for just a minute. Like every new skill, recording reading behaviors takes practice to do quickly and automatically.

spends its life working and building. As soon as a beaver leaves its family, it has much work to do.

First, the beaver must build a dam. It uses sticks, leaves, and mud to block a stream. The beaver uses its two front teeth to get the sticks. The animal uses its large flat tail to pack mud into place. A pond forms behind the dam. The beaver spends most of its life near this pond.

In the middle of the beaver's pond is a large mound. This mound of mud and twigs is the beaver's lodge or house. The beaver's family is safe in the lodge because it is well hidden. The doorway to the lodge is under the water. After the lodge is built, the beaver still cannot rest. More trees must be cut down to be used as food for the coming winter. Sometimes there will be no more trees around the pond. Then the beaver has to find trees elsewhere. These trees will have to be carried to the pond. The beaver might build canals leading deep into the forest.

All this work changes the land. As trees are cut down, birds, squirrels, and other animals may have to find new homes. Animals that feed on trees lose their food supply. The pond behind the dam floods part of the ground. Animals that used to live there have to move.

An upper-grade text with running record marks.

RUNNING RECORD CODING CONVENTIONS

Student responses are recorded above the line. The actual text and teacher interventions are below the line.

Behavior	Example	Scoring
Accurate	✓ ✓ ✓ ✓	No Error
Repetition For longer repetitions, draw a line back to beginning of rerun	✓ ✓ ✓ R ← ✓ ✓ ✓ ✓ ✓ ✓ R	No Error
Substitution Text: I love dogs.	✓ $\frac{\text{like}}{\text{love}}$ ✓	Error
Self-correction Student notices error and corrects it.	$\frac{\text{won't}}{\text{can't}}$ sc	No Error
Omission Text: A little boy	✓ $\frac{—}{\text{little}}$ ✓	Error
Insertion Text: A brown dog	✓ $\frac{\text{big}}{—}$ ✓	Error
Problem-solving Record "sounding-out behaviors."	$\frac{\text{w...e...n...✓}}{\text{went}}$	No Error
Appeal Reader looks to teacher for help, verbally or nonverbally.	$\frac{\text{A}}{\text{crunch}}$	No Error
Told Refrain from using, if possible, unless progress has stopped.	crunch T	Error

Note Omission of a proper noun is only counted as an error once. Other errors are counted every time.

Level 1 Analysis: Determining Accuracy Rate

Once you've recorded the child's reading behaviors, you can determine his or her accuracy rate. As shown in the coding chart on page 15, some behaviors count as errors, and some do not. For scoring, follow these guidelines:

○ A substitution counts as one error, no matter how many different incorrect words the student tries for the actual word.

○ Omitted words, inserted words, and words the teacher tells the student count as one error each.

○ Repetitions and self-corrections are not errors.

To determine the accuracy percentage, count the number of words in the passage, not including the title. Subtract the number of errors from the number of words, divide by the number of total words, and multiply by 100.

For example, if a text has 112 words and Sonia makes 7 errors, we would figure her accuracy by doing the following calculation:

112 total words – 7 errors = 105 correct words

105 correct words ÷ 112 total words = 93.75 accuracy rate

Score her accuracy as 94% (I always round to the nearest whole number)

This accuracy rate is useful to determine whether a book is easy, too hard, or just right for instruction (see page 12). If you know the reading level of the book used for assessment, you can assign the student a level or group children together for instruction. Students who can read books of approximately the same difficulty can likely work together in guided reading groups.

While a running record can easily be taken on a blank piece of paper, I prefer to use the form shown on page 17 when I will be using the information to make decisions about a student's reading level or to communicate with parents. I record the student's accuracy percentage and the instructional level of the text in the top section of the form. I also like to give a general description of the child's fluency with the text. I check one of the three descriptors at the top for an informal assessment of fluency. (You'll find detailed information on assessing and teaching reading fluency in Chapter 4.) The large section just below is to code the student's reading behavior. We'll address the other columns on the recording sheet in the next section.

RUNNING RECORD

Name _____ Date _____

Text _____ Level _____ ❑ Familiar ❑ Unfamiliar

Score Words correct _____   Accuracy _____%   ❑ Independent
       ——————————   ❑ Instructional
       Running words   ❑ Frustration

Fluency: ❑ Fluent with expression   ❑ Choppy   ❑ Word by word

Page	Text	E	E MSV	SC	SC MSV

Retelling	Complete	Adequate	Limited	Comments
Characters				
Plot Events				
Setting				
Main Idea				

After your student has finished reading the text, you may want to check his or her comprehension. In some cases, students read a text accurately, but don't comprehend the text. When administering a running record to younger students, ask them to retell what they read. You can record information in the Retelling section on the bottom of the form. When using an Informal Reading Inventory you may use the comprehension questions that usually accompany the text, or ask the students to retell the selection, prompting as necessary. See Chapter 5 for more information on using retellings for assessing comprehension.

Level 2 Analysis: Looking Closely at Errors

Now it's time to take a look at the errors and self-corrections your student made while reading. Analyzing these will give you a lot of information about how he or she approaches a text and the kinds of cues he or she uses to read.

When we read, we use three main sources of information. We use cues for *meaning*, or what makes sense, *language structure*, or how oral and book language sound, and *visual* information, or how a word looks. As children develop reading skills, they learn to use all three kinds of information as they read. In different stages of reading development, children may rely more heavily on one kind of information than another. Early readers, for example, often rely heavily on their memory of a story to read a text. What they "read" may have very little similarity to the actual words on the page, but it carries the idea of the story. They are using meaning cues. Other children may work very hard to sound out words, sometimes coming up with a sentence that doesn't make much sense. They are using visual information. As teachers, we want to help students use all three information systems together.

Analyzing a student's errors can give you an indication of which of these three cuing systems the student is using most, and how well all three are being integrated. Again, Marie Clay discusses this much further in her book. Yetta Goodman and Carolyn Burke also have a very thorough discussion on analyzing errors ("miscues") in *Reading Miscue Inventory Manual: Procedure for Diagnosis and Evaluation* (1972) and their newer text, *Reading Miscue Inventory: From Evaluation to Instruction* (2005). Much of their work describes older students, and is very helpful when giving an IRI. The analysis procedure is the same for both an IRI and a running record.

If you are going to use this level of analysis, you will want to use the form on page 17 for recording your running record. It will make analyzing

Error	Cues used MSV	Self-correction	Cues used MSV

✂ ....

Error	Cues used MSV	Self-correction	Cues used MSV

the errors more efficient. Alternately, you may elect to simply transfer all the errors and self-corrections to the Recording Form for IRI on page 19. This may be the best solution for your analysis of errors when using an informal reading inventory.

Whichever form you decide to use, the analysis is the same. First, take a look at each error your student made, and ask yourself, "What may have caused the student to make this error? Which of the three informational sources did he or she seem to be relying on?" Here are some things to look at when deciding.

○ **Meaning** When the child appears to be using meaning cues, or information, the attempt makes sense up to the point of error. It may be the child is using background knowledge, sentence meaning, or pictures to attempt the word. For example, if the child says *pony* instead of the accurate *horse*, he or she is likely relying on meaning cues. His or her error makes sense.

○ **Structure** When the language sounds right, or makes grammatical sense up to the point of error, the child may be using structure to determine the word. Structure is often closely related to sentence meaning. For example, if the child reads, "Sally wanted to buy hamburgers," instead of the actual text, "Sally wanted to buy her brother . . ." he or she is probably using sentence structure along with what makes sense up to the point of the error, *her brother*. The sentence that the child has constructed here suggests that Sally wants to buy *something*.

○ **Visual information** When the child's error looks similar to the correct word, he or she is probably relying on visual information. The word may begin with the same letter, or have the same letters within the word. For example, if the child substitutes *want* for *went*, it is likely a visual error. Many children confuse the words *said /is* and *of/for*. Although the words do not begin with the same letter, visual features of the words cause confusion for students. Visual errors look somewhat like the actual text.

For each error, take a look at the original word and the child's substitution, omission, or insertion. Write *MSV* next to the error. If the child seemed to be using meaning when he or she made the error, circle the *M* on the running record form. If the child was using sentence structure, circle the *S*. And if he or she was relying on visual information, circle the *V*. In some cases, you may circle all three letters. For example, if the child read the text this way, he or she would likely be using all three sources of information:

✓ ✓ ✓ ✓ ✓ <u>home</u>
The dog ran to his house.

The word *home* makes sense, it sounds right, and it has many visual similarities to the word *house*.

If you are using the IRI recording form, you will need to have the text of the IRI handy, as you can't always tell if the word makes sense or sounds right without reading the sentence.

Don't spend a huge amount of time analyzing each error. Sometimes it is very difficult to tell just what caused a student to make a substitution. It is not important that you get the perfect analysis each time. You are looking for patterns of errors, rather than worrying about one particular item.

After you have analyzed the errors, take a look at any self-corrections the child made. Using the same categories of information, ask yourself what caused the child to make the correction. For instance, in the above example, if the child had then corrected *home* and said *house*, we could guess that he or she used further visual information to make the correction. If a child had originally said *horse* for *house* and corrected the error, we could guess that he or she was using meaning to correct the error.

Once you have analyzed each error and self-correction in this way, take a look at the patterns in the child's responses. You are looking for some hints about the information the student is relying on most heavily and which he or she is not using as much. Our goal is to have students using all three sources of information as they read.

Let's look at a couple of examples. John, the first-grade student who was assessed at right, had read this text once before. As you can see, John scored 92 percent on accuracy, making this text his instructional level. His reading was fluent and

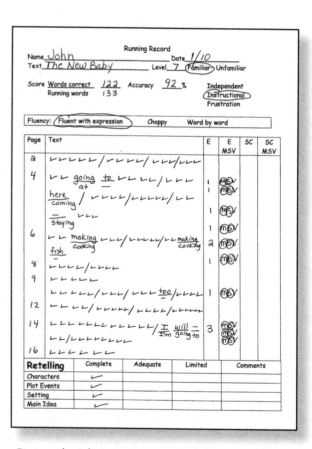

First grader John's running record of *The New Baby*

he used expression. He made 11 errors, all of which suggested that he used meaning and structure cues. He ignored the visual information, inserting words and omitting words, but making sense each time. He made no self-corrections. John's retelling was complete. He knew what was going on in the story.

The assessment below shows a reading of the same text by a different student. Although the accuracy rate is the same, the error patterns are quite different.

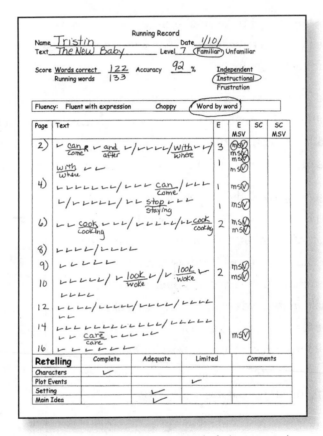

First grader Tristin's running record of *The New Baby*

Tristin made nine errors, but unlike John, she ignored the meaning cues for all but one of these errors. Her errors did not sound right or make sense, but had visual similarities. Her reading was delivered word by word and she gave a much weaker retelling. She did not understand the story as well as John did.

Based on the information in these running records, I would design very different instruction for these students. Both students have an instructional level of 7, but the way they use information is very different. John needs to use more visual information, and Tristin needs to develop strategies for using meaning cues.

Let's take a look at an older reader. Fourth grader Andrew read a text with 120 words. I've used the shorter IRI recording form (page 19) to show the errors and self-corrections he made (see below). His total of four uncorrected errors indicates this text was at his independent level (97 percent). Five of his errors made sense and were structurally correct. His fifth error came in this sentence: *Tony Hawk competed in nearly every major contest.* Andrew read, "*Tony Hawk competed in the every major contest.*" At the end of the sentence, Andrew noticed *the* did not sound right in the sentence so he reread and corrected that error by using structure meaning, and visual clues.

On closer examination of his second and third errors, it seems that Andrew did not read completely through the words, and ignored the endings. This observation gives me an instructional focus for phonics. He also was unable to decode *major* and *loop*, which may indicate some other phonics troubles. It may also indicate a limited vocabulary. I would do further testing on Andrew in the area of vocabulary and phonics skills.

	Error	Cues used MSV	Self-correction	Cues used MSV
1	the/his	M S	✓	V
2	skateboarder/ skateboard	M S V		
3	has/had	M S V		
4	his/the	M S	✓	V
5	the/nearly	M S	✓	M S V
6	manjer/major	V		
7	lop—floop/loop	V		

Fourth grader Andrew's IRI record

Analyzing errors and self-correction patterns gives me an idea of further assessments I might do with students to get a clearer picture of their reading abilities, and even some instructional ideas. But let's look at one more level of analysis you can do with a record of a student's reading.

Level 3 Analysis: Strategy Use

There is another kind of information available in an IRI or running record. The behaviors you observe and code, such as rereading, repetition, and omissions, can give you an idea about the reading strategies the child is using.

Strategies are processes that readers use to read. The strategies are mental processes, so they are not always observable, but we can guess students are using them by the way they behave. Proficient readers use many different strategies to make meaning from print.

Beginning readers use these early reading strategies:

- Directionality, including left to right movement across the page, and return sweep

- One-to-one matching of written and spoken words

- Locating known words within a text

- Locating unknown words within a text

The student's behavior while reading can let you know if he or she is using these strategies.

○ **Directionality** Watch to see if students are beginning on the left side of the page. Asking them to point to words with their fingers, and watching the movement will help you see if they are using directionality on the page. It's a little tougher to see if they are moving through individual words from left to right. Listen to any attempts they make to sound out words to see if they begin with the first letters.

○ **One-to-one matching** Noticing whether children omit or insert words can provide you with evidence about one-to-one matching. Our earlier example of the student reading

"Run, run, as fast as you can,
You won't catch me
'cause I'm the gingerbread boy"

suggests a problem with one-to-one matching. The child inserted a word, and did not notice it. Other signs of difficulty with one-to-one matching include students pointing to the text, but not actually pointing to the word they are saying out loud. Many times, the student hops over some words, or "doesn't come out even" at the end of the line, ending up with words left over or not enough words. Sometimes students will go back and reread to try to fix the problem.

○ **Locating known words** Having some known sight words within a text also contributes to one-to-one matching. For example, knowing the word *the* can help students get their fingers in the right place for sentences such as "He ran over to the house." This seems to be especially important when a line of text has some multisyllabic words in it. Often, students give each syllable of a word a touch. With the example sentence, the child would have counted *over* as two words, one for each syllable. Recognizing the known word *the* can help him anchor his finger in the text. You might see students stop and go back several times so that they are pointing to words they know as they read a sentence. If a student is reading previously known words correctly, we can guess that he or she is locating the words. After reading, you can also ask students to locate some words they know.

○ **Locating unknown words** It is useful for students to notice words that they don't already know. They can then use one of the sources of information to determine the word. I often ask students to go back to a word that they read correctly that I'm sure they did not previously know, and ask them how they figured the word out. Their answers, such as, "I checked the picture and there is a horse right there," can help me guess what they are thinking about when they come to new words. You will see students stop and check the pictures on pages, or begin sounding out words that they don't know. Sometimes they will go back and reread, or cover part of a word with their finger to try and look for a "chunk."

As readers develop, other reading strategies become important. These include:

○ **Monitoring, or noticing when something is not right** You might observe students stopping, repeating a word, or rereading a whole section of text.

○ **Searching for more information** Again, after monitoring, you might observe students rereading or looking at a picture. They might try to sound out a word.

A Word of Caution

Before you analyze information cues and the strategies a child is using, check that his or her reading is at least 90 percent accurate. Often, when students are overwhelmed by a great number of difficult words, they are unable to use strategies effectively, and they give up. You will not get a true picture of their abilities with text that is too hard.

○ **Self-correcting** Students notice a mistake, search for more information, and make another try that fits.

○ **Cross-checking, or using two or more sources of information to determine a word** Students who self-correct are usually using a second type of information to change their initial reading, such as how Andrew did when he changed his first attempt, *the*, to the correct word, *nearly*, by noticing it did not fit structurally into the sentence. Often students who are reading accurately are using multiple sources of information as they read. We just can't see it from their overt behavior.

Let's take a look at two readers reading the same text and see what we can tell about the reading strategies they are using.

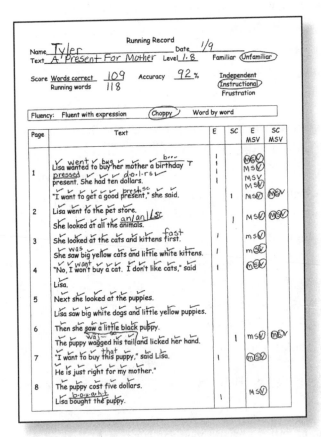

Second grader Tyler relies heavily on visual cues.

The running record above was taken for a book Tyler had read one time. The text is included to make analysis a little easier. Ordinarily, this page would just have the coding on it. In this example, Tyler's accuracy indicates the text is at his instructional level, 92 percent. We can see some evidence that he is using all three information sources in a few of his errors, although he seems to be relying on visual information and ignoring meaning in most cases.

On page 1, with the error of *pressed* for *present* and subsequent self-correction, we see evidence of monitoring, and of searching as he went back to reread. We can also see that he corrected his error by paying attention to the meaning and looking more closely at the end of the word.

On page 6, Tyler first tried *waje* for *wagged*, again relying heavily on visual information to sound out the word. He ultimately self-corrected as he read on, using the meaning of the sentence to help him out.

The last error was caused by relying upon visual clues. Tyler tried to sound out the word *brought*, and when he was unsuccessful in making a correct word, he simply moved on. In this case, meaning didn't help him out.

Notice that when I told him the word *birthday* in the first line, I was left with very little information about his behavior on difficult words. He made just the initial sound of *birthday* and then waited. In the interest of getting him started, I told him the word. But I wish I hadn't. I missed an opportunity to find out more about what strategies he uses.

Overall, Tyler showed evidence of some monitoring, searching, cross-checking, and self-correcting, but not very much. He appeared to rely heavily on visual cues for initial information (sounding out), and occasionally used meaning to self-correct. Several of his errors did not make sense (*bug/buy*, *pressed/present*, *was/saw*, *want/won't*). Considering these errors and the last error he made, where he did not try further to come up with a real word, I was concerned about his comprehension. I planned to watch closely in subsequent running records to see if he repeated the pattern of not using meaning to cross-check words.

For Tyler, my prompts and interventions will focus on helping him to develop strategies for using meaning to monitor more consistently. He made several errors that just didn't make sense, but did nothing to indicate that he noticed. I will include him in group lessons on self-correction and cross-checking strategies to help Tyler make further progress in reading. I will also help him develop some comprehension strategies. Chapter 5 includes more information on how to assess and teach comprehension.

> **Remember!**
>
> Every error is an opportunity to learn about how a reader solves problems.

Now let's take a look at another reader, who exhibits very different behaviors and strategies.

Second grader Sandy relies primarily on meaning and structure cues.

As you can see from Sandy's running record, her accuracy rate indicates that this text is at her instructional level, 91 percent. Sandy made three self-corrections, and she did so based on structure and visual information. For almost every error that Sandy made, she was ignoring visual information. Every one of her errors sounded right and made sense, but did not match visually, except for *waggled*. She inserted and omitted words. At two points, she reread when it did not sound right to say "I will to" and "she went at," and self-corrected, evidently using structure cues. On her final self-correction, Sandy made an unsuccessful attempt to sound out the word *bought* and continued reading. She ultimately reread and self-corrected based on the meaning of the sentence.

Sandy shows evidence of monitoring, searching, and cross-checking, primarily with structure and meaning. She tends to ignore visual information.

The kind of instruction that will benefit her is very different from that which will help Tyler. My prompts for Sandy will focus on checking to see if her words match and look right to help her integrate visual information into her reading. She may need to improve her phonics skills or her vocabulary. For more information on assessing phonics and ways to effectively teach word-solving strategies, take a look at Chapter 2. For more information on vocabulary and sight words, see Chapter 3.

So we've seen how to assess students to determine reading levels, their use of information in a text, and the reading strategies they use. Once we've gathered this information, it's time to design some lessons.

The time you spend collecting data about your students' reading levels and use of text will be time well spent, as it helps you design a course of action to help your readers succeed.

Begin by finding the right reading level for each child. You will want texts that are neither too easy nor too hard so that students can be fully engaged in and not bored or overwhelmed by the text. A text at their instructional level is also one in which they can practice the skills you've taught them. Use the first information (Level 1 data) you collect to form guided reading groups (groups of students reading at approximately the same level). I use a chart like the one shown at the top of page 30 to record my class's instructional levels.

I group students into ranges to form reading groups of three to five students, ideally. The levels across the top of the chart will, of course, be different based on your grade level. This chart happens to reflect the levels of some students in a first-grade class. As you can see, there is a wide range of ability levels among these students. Grouping by level allows me to use the most appropriate texts for each group—not too easy or too hard.

Level 1 Data

Student	3 and below	4—6	7—9	10 and above
Duncan			9	
George		6		
Johnny				12
Julia		5		
Julio				11
Justin		5		
McKenzie			8	
Stacy	3			
Sylvette	2			
Tommy	2			
Tristin			7	

Next, I make a similar chart to see what kinds of information students are using as they read (see below). This will help me to determine lessons not only for small groups, but for the whole group and individuals, as well. For example, very few of the students on this chart are consistently using all three cuing systems. The whole class would benefit from teacher-directed lessons to encourage cross-checking to see that reading makes sense, sounds right, and looks right, too.

Level 2 Data

Student	Often uses meaning	Often uses structure	Often uses visual
Duncan	✓	✓	✓
George	✓	✓	
Johnny	✓	✓	
Julia			✓
Julio	✓	✓	✓
Justin			✓
McKenzie			✓
Stacy	✓	✓	
Sylvette	✓		
Tommy	✓	✓	
Tristin			✓

Finally, one last chart, below, will record the strategies that students appear to be using.

Level 3 Data

Student	Left to right	One-to-one	Known words	Unknown words	Monitor	Search	Self-correct	Cross-check
Duncan	✓	✓	✓	✓	✓		✓	✓
George	✓	✓	✓	✓	✓		✓	
Johnny	✓	✓	✓	✓	✓	✓	✓	✓
Julia	✓	✓	✓					
Julio	✓	✓	✓	✓	✓	✓	✓	✓
Justin	✓	✓	✓	✓		✓		
McKenzie	✓	✓	✓	✓	✓			✓
Stacy	✓	✓	✓					
Sylvette	✓							
Tommy	✓							
Tristin	✓	✓	✓	✓	✓			

Note Older students will most likely have the first four beginning strategies in place, so you may not need to include them on your chart.

Cross-reference all three charts to find patterns. Students at the lowest levels, including Stacy, Sylvette, and Tommy, are liable to be missing one-to-one matching, and are probably relying a great deal on meaning and structure as they read. At the higher levels, groups of students relying on one kind of information or another will become evident, for example, Julia, Justin, Tristin, and McKenzie rely heavily on visual information when reading and are not doing much self-correcting. It may be that students are always cross-checking a particular source of information second, as Sandy did in the running record shown on page 28. Notice that George self-corrects, but uses meaning and structure cues, rather than visual cues to do so. With the charts, we can plan our instruction for individuals and small and large groups.

These beginning charts are just that—a beginning. The profile of each student and your class may change quickly. Ongoing assessment is key. It's a good idea to take a running record of your struggling students at least every two weeks. You will want to know if your reading levels are appropriate, and if your instruction is making a difference in terms of the strategies and information your students are using. Your most capable students can probably wait for every four or five weeks. Midrange students would benefit from an informal check every three weeks or so.

TEACH

Just as there are different levels of analysis, there will be different kinds of instruction for your students—whole-group, small-group, and individual work. You can support students as they try out different strategies in the context of read-alouds, shared reading, and guided reading. For example, as you read aloud to first-grade students, you can make an error and stop. You might say something like this:

"You know, that doesn't sound quite right to me. Let me look at that word again. Yes, it starts like *kitten*, and ends the same way, but it doesn't make sense to say, '*Mom was in the kitten*,' does it? When I check the picture, I can see Mom. She's standing by the refrigerator. I bet that word is *kitchen*. Let me look again—oh yes, there's the *ch* in the middle. I didn't notice that before. It's important that my words look right and make sense, too. Now, let me reread that whole page so I can remember what is happening."

You've effectively modeled monitoring, searching, cross-checking, and self-correction in just a moment.

For older students, you can do the same thing, particularly modeling strategies for monitoring with meaning. For example, "The text says, '*I saw the pine trees ignite.*' I'm not quite sure what that means, so I think I will read on a little bit and see if that helps. It says, '*Then I saw everyone stampede to get away from the fire.*' Oh, *ignite* must mean to catch on fire. In the picture on the next page, I can see some trees burning, so I bet I'm right. Sometimes you just have to read a little farther and you can figure out what words mean. Checking those pictures can help a lot, too."

One of the most effective instructional practices you can use is coaching your students while they are reading. I compare this to teaching my son to drive. I could have talked to him a lot about what he needed to do before he got into the car, but the most effective time for me to discuss being a defensive driver was when he got behind the wheel. It's a lot easier to think about what that other driver might be doing when you can see him, and Nathan got a chance to try things out and see how they worked.

It's the same with reading. If you can sit with a child while he or she is reading text, you can prompt the child to try out the strategies that you have previously modeled in small- or large-group settings. The chart below will give you some ideas for prompting students to use different sources of information and strategies while reading.

Coaching Statements and Activities to Use

If the child . . .	then you might say . . .	Activities to try
ignores meaning cues	Did that make sense? What do you think the author might say there? Try that again and think about what makes sense. Check the picture.	● Comprehension activities, including read-aloud/modeling, Chapter 5
ignores language structure cues	Can we say it that way? Does that sound like the way we talk? Does that sound right? How do you think an author might say that? Try that again and make it sound like the way we talk. How would we ask that?	● Guess the Covered Word, Chapter 3 ● Cloze Passages, Chapter 3 ● Language Experience, Chapter 5 ● Picture Walk, Chapter 5
ignores visual cues	Does that look right? How does it start? What part of the word do you know? Do you know another word like that? It could be, but check the middle, end, and beginning. If it were ____, what letters would you expect to see? (Cover the word while you ask this one.) Reread it and get your mouth ready with the first sounds. Do you see all the letters you need for that word? Do you see any chunks, prefixes, or word parts that can help you?	● Teach phonics strategies, Chapter 2 ● Develop sight vocabulary and specific reading vocabulary, Chapter 3

Coaching Statements and Activities to Use

If the child . . .	then you might say . . .	Activities to try
does not have directionality	Can you find the starting place?	Place a green sticky dot for a starting place on the page.
does not have one-to-one matching	Try that again and make it match. Read it with your finger. Did it come out even? Did you have enough (or too many) words? Was you finger under the word when you said it?	• Be the Sentence, Chapter 2 • Language Experience, Chapter 5 • Teach sight words to serve as anchors, Chapter 3
does not locate known words	Can you find a word you know? Did you see the word ____? Read it again and see if you see some words you know. Look for some words that will help you.	• Book introduction to locate known words, Chapter 5 • Develop sight vocabulary, Chapter 3
does not notice new words	Did you see a tricky part? Where is the hard part? Can you find a new word? Do you see something new?	• Book introduction to locate new words, Chapter 5 • Develop sight vocabulary, Chapter 3
does not monitor	Were you right? (Say this sometimes when they are right as well as when they are wrong.) How do you know? You made a mistake on this page. Can you find it? Why are you stopping? What's wrong? You found out something was wrong all by yourself. Check that part. You said ____. What's wrong with that? • Also try these silent prompts: ○ Point to wrong word and stop. ○ Wait for him or her to see if he or she can find the error.	• Cloze Passages, Chapter 3 • Guess the Covered Word, Chapter 3 • Comprehension activities, Chapter 5

Coaching Statements and Activities to Use

If the child . . .	then you might say . . .	Activities to try
does not search	What else might help you? What else can you try? Is there anything else on the page that can help? Does that match the picture, too? Does that look right, too? Does that make sense, too? Does that sound right, too? What can you do to help yourself? Will this help? (Point to a helpful cue.)	● Guess the Covered Word, Chapter 3 ● Encourage the use of picture clues, Chapter 5
does not cross-check	Does it look right and make sense, too? It could be, but what else will make sense (or sound right, look right)? Did you reread to see if you were right? How do you know you are right? Do you know you are right two ways?	● Guess the Covered Word, Chapter 3 ● Teach decoding skills, Chapter 2 ● Comprehension activities, Chapter 5
does not self-correct	Something isn't quite right. Try that again. There's something wrong on this page. Can you find it? Use everything you know. Is there anything else you can try? You're so close. Try it once more. Was that okay? You fixed that all by yourself! You noticed something was wrong. Why did you stop?	● Phonics activities, Chapter 2 ● Comprehension activities, Chapter 5

The coaching statements will help you encourage individual students to use strategies and information sources. The activities will help to teach students strategies and ways to use phonics, vocabulary, fluency, and comprehension. The initial data you've collected from the IRI and running record will give you a good beginning, but you will need more information about your students to effectively plan your instruction. The remainder of this book includes further assessments in these areas and how to use them to plan for individual and group needs.

Resources and Further Reading

Beaver, J. & Carter, M. (2006). *Developmental reading assessment (2nd ed.).* Parsippany, NJ: Celebration Press.

Clay, M. (1993). *An observation survey of early literacy achievement.* Portsmouth, NH: Heinemann.

Fountas, I. C. & Pinnell, G. S. (2007). *Fountas & Pinnell benchmark assessment system (grades K—2 and 3–6).* Portsmouth, NH: Heinemann.

Goodman, Y. & Burke, C. L. (1972). *Reading miscue inventory manual: Procedure for diagnosis and evaluation.* New York: MacMillan.

Goodman, Y. Watson, D., Burke, C. L., & Cambourne, B. (2005). *Reading miscue inventory: From evaluation to instruction.* Katonah, NY: Richard C. Owens.

Rasinski, T. V. & Padak, N. (2005). *3-minute reading assessments (grades 1–4 and grades 5–8).* New York: Scholastic.

Rasinski, T. V. & Padak, N. (2007). *3-minute reading assessments: A professional development DVD and study guide (grades 1–8).* New York: Scholastic.

Silvaroli, N. J. & Wheelock, W. H. (2001). *Classroom reading inventory (9th ed.).* New York: McGraw Hill.

Wilde, S. (2000). *Miscue analysis made easy: Building on student strengths.* Portsmouth, NH: Heinemann.

Chapter 2

Phonemic Awareness and Phonics

Classroom Snapshot

Allen is a second-grade boy in a remedial reading program. His teacher from last year reports that he did pretty well for the first part of first grade, and then began to struggle. Now when Allen reads, he makes many errors. The words he misreads often begin and end with the same letters as the printed words on the page. These substitutions usually make sense in the text, but not always. Sometimes when Allen comes to an unfamiliar word, he stops and searches the pictures, and goes back and re-reads the preceding text. Then he slowly and painstakingly makes a sound for every letter in the unfamiliar word, but cannot put them together. He moves on, even though his hard work has not resulted in an actual word. Allen's teacher reports his spelling is also very poor. He leaves out letters, uses incorrect letters to represent sounds, and writes letters in the wrong order.

Allen is struggling in both reading and writing. In first grade, he learned to use picture and meaning cues as well as some beginning sounds to read easier text. Using these basic skills in combination, Allen was able to successfully figure out the text of simple stories. But Allen is struggling now that the texts he reads contain more unfamiliar words. He doesn't have the tools to figure out, or decode, them. Allen needs phonics instruction.

This chapter will discuss the important role of phonemic awareness and phonics in reading. We will look at how decoding skills develop, offer some ways to assess students' proficiency, and look at research-supported instructional strategies you can use for individuals and groups.

What Are Phonemic Awareness and Phonics?

Phonemic awareness is the ability to hear and manipulate the sounds of our language orally. Phonics is the relationship between those sounds and the letters used to spell them. Students first have to be able to isolate and recognize sounds and then identify the letters that represent those sounds in order to read unfamiliar words.

Learning to read in English is not an easy task. There are 41 phonemes, or distinct sounds, in the English language, and, of course, only 26 letters. There are multiple ways that phonemes, or individual sounds, can be spelled. For example, the sound we refer to as "long a" (as in *take*) can be represented by the letter *a* followed by an *e* at the end of the word, as in this example. But it can also be spelled with *ai* as in *rain*, *eigh* as in *eight* and *ay* as in *day*. Sometimes the final *e* is dropped, such as when *take* becomes *taking*. Readers trying to effectively use sound-letter correspondences face further challenges because the same letters don't always represent the same sound, as in the sound represented by *ou* in the words *could*, *though*, *cough*, *house*, *group*, and *touch*. Finally, homographs, or words that are spelled alike but have different meanings and pronunciations based on context, such as "It took less than a *minute* to read the *minute* note," create even more difficulties for readers.

Some words are not phonetically regular. That is, they are not pronounced in the same way as other words with a similar letter pattern. *The*, one of the most common words, is a good example. If we look at other words with similar spellings, like *she*, *he*, and *be*, we can see that if *the* followed the pattern, it would be pronounced with the same "long e" sound the other words have. These phonetically irregular words are called sight words and are generally learned through memorization. Chapter 3 includes a discussion of ways to assess students' knowledge of sight words and activities for teaching them.

Students can't memorize every word. Eventually, they must "break the code" and understand that letters represent sounds and those sounds blend together to make words. Students must have the ability to quickly decode unfamiliar words using phonics as a tool. Students who decode slowly read slowly and often have comprehension problems.

What Does Research Say About Phonemic Awareness and Phonics?

Phonemic awareness and letter knowledge have been identified as the two best school-entry predictors of how well children will learn to read during their first two years in school (*Report of the National Reading Panel,* 2000). Given this data, the National Reading Panel analyzed 96 published instructional comparisons to determine whether *teaching* phonemic awareness actually improved students' reading abilities. The panel found that phonemic awareness instruction helped all types of children in reading, with improvements in both word reading and comprehension. Their report states that phonemic awareness instruction is more effective when it is taught with written letters and in small, focused groups that include explicit instruction in how to apply phonemic awareness skills in reading and writing tasks. These findings indicate that we do not need to teach phonemic awareness completely separate from phonics. We don't have to wait to introduce letters until all aspects of phonemic awareness have been mastered.

The *Report of the National Reading Panel* also summarized the findings of 38 research studies concerning phonics instruction, and made several recommendations. First, the panel found that explicit and sequential teaching of phonics is more beneficial than programs that do not teach phonics. The report defines explicit and sequential teaching as a program that systematically teaches "the full array of letter-sound correspondences" (page 2-99), including consonants, long and short vowel sounds, and vowel and consonant digraphs, such as *oi, ou, sh, ch,* and *th.* It may also include word chunks such as *–ack, –ill,* and *–op.*

Second, the report indicated that there is no difference in effectiveness between the four major types of phonics instruction programs:

- **Synthetic phonics,** or converting letters into sounds and blending the sounds to form words in isolation

- **Analytic phonics,** or analyzing letter-sound relationships in known words rather than pronouncing sounds in isolation

- **Phonics in context,** or using sound-letter correspondences with context cues to identify unfamiliar words in text

- **Analogy phonics,** or using parts of words already known to identify new words

Some effective programs combine two or more of the approaches.

Students must understand certain concepts about letters and the sounds they make to successfully decode an unfamiliar word. The following are some of the basic ideas that students must learn:

- Letters represent sounds
- Letters combine to make words
- Two consonants can form a single sound (*ch*, *sh*, *th*)
- Two or more consonants can make a blended sound (*pl*, *spr*)
- Consonants can be silent (*kn*, *wr*)
- Consonants can represent more than one sound (*g*, *c*)
- Vowel letters can represent more than one sound (short, long, other)
- Vowels can be silent (*lik*e)
- Two vowels can form a single long sound (*ee*, *oa*)
- Two vowels can form a new sound (*oi*, *oo*)
- The letter r can change a vowel sound (*ar*, *er*)
- Prefixes, suffixes, and endings can be added to words or word parts
- Long words can be divided into syllable chunks, each with its own vowel sound

Third, the report stated that phonics teaching is a means to an end. Children need phonemic awareness in order to blend sounds together to decode words and break spoken words into their parts to write words. Children should understand that the purpose of learning letter-sound relationships is to apply this knowledge in reading and writing. Phonics instruction should not dominate a reading program, but be integrated with other components to create a balanced reading program. It's a piece, albeit an important one.

So it is important that we teach phonics, and no method is more effective than another. How do we know what to teach students?

First, let's look at an assessment for phonemic awareness, and then some methods for assessing phonics skills.

The assessment tools and analyses that follow are in two parts: Phonemic Awareness Assessments for emergent and beginning readers and Phonics Assessments for developing readers.

Phonemic Awareness Assessments

Phonemic awareness encompasses many different oral skills. It is all about being able to hear and use sounds. If students can't use sounds orally, it will be difficult for them to do similar tasks with print. While we can include printed letters in our instruction, when we assess phonemic awareness we will get more accurate results if we begin with oral assessments before moving to written symbols.

First, students must be able to identify individual words within sentences, for example, determining that the sentence *I like to eat watermelon* is five words. Once children can identify word boundaries, they should be able to count the number of syllables within a word, for example, breaking *watermelon* into four syllables. They should also be able to use rhyming words and identify words that sound the same at the end; students should be able to correctly answer "Which word rhymes with *like—bike* or *book*?" Rhyming is an important skill for students, especially if you will be teaching phonics by analogy.

Next, children need to be able to recognize specific sounds and their locations within orally spoken words, for example, "What's the sound that starts these words—*ball, book, bell*?" We often talk with children about the beginning sounds of words. As we teach reading, we say, "This letter represents the sound at the beginning of *dog*." If we don't find out whether children are able to isolate the beginning of orally spoken words and discriminate the sounds, our instruction is useless, and likely confusing.

It is also important to determine whether students are able to blend individual sounds together to create words, for example, "/m/. . ./a/. . ./n/ says *man*," and stretch out words to hear the individual phonemes, for example, "What are the sounds in *go*?" These two skills are vital for reading and spelling, respectively.

Finally, we want to know if students can mentally manipulate words by adding and subtracting sounds, for example, "If I add /d/ to *rip*, I get *drip*!" This skill is very important if students will be learning to decode by analogy.

Once you've assessed students' phonemic awareness skills, you will want to assess their knowledge about letters and the sounds they can represent. But first, let's look at some assessments for their oral skills.

PHONEMIC AWARENESS TASK

The first assessment (page 42) is a tool to assess students' abilities with rhyming, identifying beginning and ending sounds, blending and manipulating sounds, and segmenting words. It is designed to be used with kindergarten or first-grade students, although you may decide to use it with struggling second graders.

Procedure

1. Give this test orally to one student at a time.

2. Record correct responses on a copy of the Phonemic Awareness Task form with a plus (+) and incorrect responses with a minus (–).

PHONEMIC AWARENESS TASK

Name _____ Date _____

Part 1 Rhyme _____/4

_____ 1. Tell me a word that rhymes with **bat**.

_____ 2. Tell me a word that rhymes with **red**.

_____ 3. Tell me a word that rhymes with **me**.

_____ 4. Tell me a word that rhymes with **make**.

Part 2 Phoneme Isolation (Beginning and Ending) _____/6

_____ 5. Tell me the first sound in **boy**.

_____ 6. Tell me the first sound in **paste**.

_____ 7. Tell me the first sound in **ring**.

_____ 8. Tell me the last sound in **back**.

_____ 9. Tell me the last sound in **ham**.

_____ 10. Tell me the last sound in **drop**.

Part 3 Phoneme Blending _____/4

_____ 11. What word is this? **h . . . op**

_____ 12. What word is this? **m . . . ouse**

_____ 13. What word is this? **r . . . a . . . n**

_____ 14. What word is this? **j . . . u . . . m . . . p**

Part 4 Phoneme Segmentation _____/4

_____ 15. Say the sounds in this word slowly: **fat** (f . . . a . . . t)

_____ 16. Say the sounds in this word slowly: **kiss** (k . . . i . . . s)

_____ 17. Say the sounds in this word slowly: **game** (g . . . a . . . m)

_____ 18. Say the sounds in this word slowly: **black** (b . . . l . . . a . . . k)

Part 5 Phoneme Deletion (Beginning) _____/3

_____ 19. What is **mat** without the /m/?

_____ 20. What is **dear** without the /d/?

_____ 21. What is **pin** without the /p/?

Part 6 Phoneme Deletion (Ending) _____/3

_____ 22. What word is **rake** without the /k/?

_____ 23. What word is **mice** without the /s/?

_____ 24. What word is **beat** without the /t/?

3. In Part 1, accept as correct nonsense rhyming words.

4. If a student does not understand a task, give an example, such as "*Car* and *bar* rhyme," for Part 1, or "The first sound of man is /m/," for Part 5. Do not give an example for the same target word or sound.

5. In parts 2 and 4, notice that the correct response is a sound, not a letter name. If a student tells you the letter name, ask what sound it represents.

LETTER IDENTIFICATION ASSESSMENT

A second assessment for your kindergarten and first-grade students is a letter identification test. It is important to find out what students know about letters, since in instruction you will be referring to them by both name and sound. The Letter Identification assessment (pages 45 and 46) is adapted from the work of Marie Clay (1993). It differs from some letter tests in that it also can be used to collect information about other ways students may know letters. The first column is for recording which letter names students know, but you can also record information about associated sounds and words that students know in the second and third columns. For example, a student may not know the name or sound of the letter *t*, but may know that it is in his friend Tom's name.

Procedure

1. Give this test to one student at a time.

2. Have available a copy of both letter identification forms.

3. Show the child the student form (page 45). Use an index card to reveal one line of letters at a time, and ask for the name of each letter. On the Letter Identification Record, mark correct responses with a check in the first column (Name). If the student is unable to say the name of the letter, ask for the sound it represents and mark correct responses with a check in the second column (Sound). If the student is unable to name the sound, ask if he or she knows a word that the letter is in, and record the word in the third column (Word). Record incorrect letter name responses in the last column (Substitution).

4. While this form was originally designed to record either name, sound, or word knowledge about letters, many teachers routinely ask for the sound of each correctly named uppercase letter. Correct responses are marked with a check in the second column. Credit is given for the short vowel

sound. If the student first provides the long sound, ask for the other, short sound. It's not necessary to check sounds for both upper- and lowercase letters, nor is it necessary to routinely ask if students know a word containing the letter if they can name the letter or sound.

5. If the student can't give any information for any letters in the first line, I locate and point to the first letter of his or her name. If the student can successfully name that letter, I continue showing other letters from his or her name, but not in sequential order.

6. If the student is unable to name any uppercase letters, you may decide to stop testing and not show the lowercase letters. Generally, knowledge of uppercase letters develops first.

7. Find out which letters students have some correct knowledge of, either by letter name, sound, or word association, and record the score (total correct out of 54 examples). Analyze the results, looking particularly at areas of confusion and knowledge of upper- and lower-case pairs.

SENTENCE DICTATION

The Sentence Dictation Record (page 49) is another adaptation from the work of Marie Clay (1993). It assesses both students' phonemic awareness and their ability to represent the sounds with letters, thus providing valuable information about how students actually work with sounds.

Sentence dictation is ideally administered individually. It can be used in small groups, if necessary, but it's much harder to see what an individual student is doing when you assess in a group and it can be difficult to record the letters students used to represent particular words. Therefore, for my most struggling readers, I do the assessment one-on-one so I can observe the strategies they use for locating sounds in words. I like to do this assessment three times a year, and for my most capable students I administer it in small groups at midyear and in the spring. In the fall, and for struggling students, I always assess individually.

Procedure

1. Provide the student with a blank piece of paper and a pencil, and make a copy of the sentence dictation form for yourself.

Letter Identification

M	F	K	P	W	Z
B	H	O	J	U	
C	Y	L	Q	A	
D	N	S	X	I	
E	G	R	V	T	
m	f	k	p	w	z
b	h	o	j	u	a
c	y	l	q	a	g
d	n	s	x	i	
e	g	r	v	t	

LETTER IDENTIFICATION RECORD

Name _____ Date _____

Grade _____   Score _____/54

	Name	Sound	Word	Substitution		Name	Sound	Word	Substitution
M					m				
F					f				
K					k				
P					p				
W					w				
Z					z				
B					b				
H					h				
O					o				
J					j				
U					u				
C					a				
Y					c				
L					y				
Q					l				
A					q				
D					a				
N					g				
S					d				
X					n				
I					s				
E					x				
G					i				
R					e				
V					g				
T					r				
					v				
					t				
			Totals						

2. Tell the student you are going to say some sentences and you want him or her to write as much of the sentence as possible. Explain, "If you aren't sure how to write a word, say the word slowly to yourself and write any letters you can hear."

3. Say the first sentence completely, and then say each word of the sentence individually. Say the words slowly, but don't stretch out the sounds. If necessary, prompt the student to think about the sounds he or she was able to hear.

4. If you are testing individually, record the letters the student is writing above the corresponding word on the recording sheet. (Each word has lines above it that correspond to the number of phonemes heard in the word.) Record how sounds are represented by writing the letter the child wrote on the line above the corresponding letter. For example, if he or she writes *have* as *hv* you will leave the line above the *a* blank. If the child writes *have* as *h*, you will leave the lines above both *a* and *v* blank. Also watch for the behaviors listed in the box and check them off if observed. The behaviors will give you information about how the child is processing the words in his or her head.

5. If you are testing in a small group, observe and check off individual behaviors, and write down the corresponding letters for words after students finish.

6. If the student is able to write at least a few sounds of the first sentence, say the second sentence slowly, and then repeat each individual word. Record the student's work. If the student is unable to accurately represent more than one sound for the first sentence, or just writes strings of letters with no attention to individual sounds, stop testing after the first sentence.

7. Score the assessment. Give credit for each sound that is accurately represented by an appropriate letter, although standard spellings may or may not be present. For example, *like* may be written *lik* or *lic*, since the *e* is silent and *c* can also represent the sound /k/. In either case, the student would receive the full three points for the word. Look for any accurate representation of the vowel and consonant sounds indicated, and circle those that the student uses correctly. You would not necessarily expect students to write the final *e* in *have, home,* or *like,* the *e* in *named,* or the final *b* in *climb.* When the student correctly uses the vowel and consonant sounds indicated, circle them. Record any accurately spelled words under "known words."

8. Analyze the assessment. Does the student hear and represent beginning and ending sounds? Which consonants are represented? Can he or she hear vowel sounds and sequence sounds in order? How was the student processing the words? Did he or she stretch the sounds or say the letter names? The answers to these questions will help you make crucial teaching decisions.

SAMPLE PHONEMIC AWARENESS ASSESSMENT ANALYSIS

Looking at these three assessments together will give you the most information about your students. You will want to carefully compare the ability to hear sounds in words, knowledge of letter names, and the ability to use this knowledge to write words. Let's take a look at the results of a first-grade student named Joe (completed assessments appear on page 50).

The Phonemic Awareness Task results tell us that Joe can generate rhyming words, identify beginning and ending sounds, and successfully blend onset and rime. He was able to blend three sounds together to make a word, but not more, and was unable to consistently segment words into separate phonemes or manipulate sounds.

Looking at Joe's Sentence Dictation assessment, we see that he successfully represents a few beginning and ending sounds, and had three known words, *I*, *a*, and *red*. Comparing this to his Letter Identification assessment, we can see that he knows the names of more letters than he can use to represent sounds. Joe knew either the capital or lowercase name of 16 letters, but only represented six of the consonant sounds when writing. Joe was not consistent with the sound /m/. He used it correctly in *home*, but not with *named* or *climb*. It's unclear if he knows the sound /r/. Although he could spell *red*, he did not tell the name of *R* or *r*, nor could he use the letter *d* to spell *named* or *dog*. The word *red* was clearly a sight word, judging from the way he quickly spelled it aloud upon hearing the word spoken. His class had learned a song in which the word was spelled out.

Occasionally, like Joe, a student will have a fairly high score on the Letter Identification assessment and lower scores on the other two tests. He knows the letter names, but cannot yet hear the sounds or use the letters to represent sounds. Simply knowing the letter names is not enough for an early reader. The student needs many opportunities to develop phonemic awareness and letter-sound relationships. See the planning chart on page 59 for instruction ideas.

Sentence Dictation Record
(Hearing and Representing Sounds in Words)

Name _____ Date _____

I have a big red dog

at home named Spot.

We like to jump and climb.

Score _____/45

    Vowel sounds: ă ā ĕ ē ĭ ī ŏ ō ŭ

    Consonant sounds: b c d g h j k l m n p r s t v w

    Known words:

Behaviors observed

    ____ Reluctant to try   ____ Stretched sounds

    ____ Random letters   ____ Named letters

    ____ Appealed

    ____ Knew sound, but not form (What does an *h* look like?)

Phonemic Awareness Task

Score 13 / 24

Name Joe   Date 9/24

Part 1: Rhyme 3 /4
- **+** 1. Tell me a word that rhymes with <u>bat</u>.
- **+** 2. Tell me a word that rhymes with <u>red</u>.
- **+** 3. Tell me a word that rhymes with <u>me</u>.
- **—** 4. Tell me a word that rhymes with <u>make</u>.

Part 2: Phoneme Isolation (Beginning and Ending) __/6
- **+** 5. Tell me the first sound in <u>boy</u>.
- **+** 6. Tell me the first sound in <u>paste</u>.
- **+** 7. Tell me the first sound in <u>ring</u>.
- **+** 8. Tell me the last sound in <u>back</u>.
- **+** 9. Tell me the last sound in <u>ham</u>.
- **+** 10. Tell me the last sound in <u>drop</u>.

Part 3: Phoneme Blending __/4
- **+** 11. What word is this? h......op
- **+** 12. What word is this? m. . . .ouse
- **+** 13. What word is this? r. . a. . .n
- **—** 14. What word is this? j...u....m....p

Part 4: Phoneme Segmentation __/4
- **+** 15. Say the sounds in this word slowly: fat (f .. a .. t)
- **—** 16. Say the sounds in this word slowly: kiss (k.. i ..s)
- **—** 17. Say the sounds in this word slowly: game (g..a ..m)
- **—** 18. Say the sounds in this word slowly: black (b...l...a...k)

Part 5: Phoneme Deletion—beginning __/3
- **—** 19. What is <u>mat</u> without the /m/?
- **—** 20. What is <u>dear</u> without the /d/?
- **—** 21. What is <u>pin</u> without the /p/?

Part 6: Phoneme Deletion—ending __/3
- **—** 22. What word is <u>rake</u> without the /k/?
- **—** 23. What word is <u>mice</u> without the /s/?
- **—** 24. What word is <u>beat</u> without the /b/?

Sentence Dictation Record
Hearing and Representing Sounds in Words

Name Joe   Date 9/25

I̲ ___ a̲ B̲__ r̲e̲d̲ ___

I have a big red dog

_I̲ __M̲ ____ S̲___

at home named Spot.

said "c" could not write

Y̲_ L̲__ t̲_ J̲___ ___ ___

We like to jump and climb.

said "c", what's a 'c' look like?

Score 12 /45

vowel sounds: ă ā ĕ ē ĭ ī ŏ ō ŭ (?)
consonant sounds: (b)c d g h (j) k (l)(m) n p r (s)(t) v w
known words: I, a, red

Behaviors observed:
- ✓ Reluctant to try *on some words (have, dog, named, climb)*
- ___ Random letters   ___ Stretched sounds
- ✓ Appealed Is that right?   ✓ Named letters r-e-d
- ___ Knew sound but not form (What's an "h" look like?) C

Letter Identification

Date 9/25   Score 31 /54
Name Joe   Grade 1

	Name	Sound	Word	Substitution		Name	Sound	Word	Substitution
M	✓				m	✓			
F	•				f	✓			
K	•				k	•			
P	✓				p	✓			
W	•				w	•			
Z	✓				z	✓		d	
B	✓				b	•			
H			Hailey		h	•			
O	✓				o	•		i	
J	✓				j	•			
U	•				u	•			
C	✓				a	ă			
Y	✓				c	✓			
L	•				y	✓			
Q	•				l			i	
A	✓				q			p	
D	✓		M		a	✓			
N	•				g	ĕ			
S	✓				d	✓		m	
X	✓				n	✓			
I	✓				s	✓			
E	✓				x	✓			
G	•				i	✓			
R	•				e	✓			
V	•				g	•			
T	✓				r			red	
					v	ø			
					t	✓			
	16	1			Totals	13		1	

Three short phonemic awareness tasks show that while this first-grade student knows letter names, he cannot yet hear the sounds or use the letters to represent sounds. (See analysis on page 48.)

On the other hand, some students have higher scores on the phonemic awareness assessment and meager knowledge of letters. They may know the sound on the sentence dictation test, but not know how to write the letter. This sometimes indicates that students have had little experience with books and words. Although they will get these opportunities in the classroom, they will need targeted instruction to learn the letter names and forms. Again, take a look at the chart later in the chapter for instruction ideas.

The three phonemic awareness assessments are appropriate to use early in the year, to provide focus for your whole-group lessons, and to design some intervention and small-group lessons. Look for patterns that are reflected in your whole class. Is rhyming difficult for most children? Then focus on those books and songs that teach rhyming. Are certain letters proving difficult for many of your children? Choose read-alouds, shared writing, and other whole-group activities to focus on those letters. Make sure to do informal assessments as you work with your students in smaller groups to see their progress. For your struggling readers, use the assessments every six weeks. For students progressing well, you may want to assess formally only in the fall and midyear. Once students have demonstrated mastery of these phonemic awareness tasks, you won't have to reassess.

For students in second grade and above, you will need to know what phonics skills they have mastered. Let's see how to find out.

Phonics Assessments

There are several ways to assess what students understand about phonics. First, you will get information as you analyze their running records, as discussed in Chapter 1. As I looked at Tyler's errors when reading *A Present for Mother* (page 26), I noticed difficulties with multisyllable words, as well as letter-by-letter sounding of the word *bought*. Right away I saw that I needed to help Tyler understand that each syllable of a word has a vowel sound, and that word parts can help him figure out unknown words. I would need to check to see if he can read any words with the *-ought* pattern. He also had troubles with the word *wagged*. He initially used the long *a* sound. I might do an informal check to see if he understands about how endings work when added to words with short vowel sounds. Analyze your own students' running records and look for patterns of visual errors.

A second source of information about phonics is your students' writing. Much of their understanding of how letters work to represent sounds can be understood by examining how they spell words. Generally, as students demonstrate control of a spelling pattern, we see that they also have control of the same pattern in reading and can use it to decode unfamiliar words. The sentence dictation assessment discussed above will let you see if your beginning readers understand how to represent all of the short vowel sounds as well as some of the long vowel sounds using a final *e*.

DEVELOPMENTAL SPELLING ASSESSMENT

For second-grade and older students, developmental spelling tests, such as the spelling inventories for primary and intermediate grades on pages 53 and 54, can be very useful. These assessments were adapted from the work of Donald R. Bear and his colleagues, as described in *Words Their Way* (2000). If you want to see if students have mastered specific spelling patterns, you may revise the list to reflect those patterns.

Administer the assessments individually or in a small group so that you will be able to monitor students' responses and notice when to stop testing. Use the primary assessment in the spring with first graders who have mastered the dictation test and with second graders. Use the intermediate grade assessment for grades 3 and up, or for primary grade students who are able to correctly spell 18 or more of the words on the primary assessment.

Procedure

1. Let students know that you will be asking them to spell some words. Explain that some words may be easy to spell and some may be more difficult. They should try to spell the word the best they can, writing down all the sounds they hear.

2. Say each word once, use the word in a sentence, and repeat the word. Do not stretch the sounds out slowly for the students, but encourage them to do so quietly on their own.

3. Work in groups of five words, with each group focusing on a different phonics component with an increasing degree of complexity. You may want to stop testing if students miss three of the five words in the group.

4. Record the results. Write a plus (+) for words spelled correctly. Record incorrect spellings after the word.

PRIMARY GRADES SPELLING INVENTORY

_____ 1. tan

_____ 2. led

_____ 3. hit

_____ 4. mop

_____ 5. gum

_____ 6. left

_____ 7. spin

_____ 8. chick

_____ 9. shop

_____ 10. ride

_____ 11. lake

_____ 12. rain

_____ 13. soap

_____ 14. peek

_____ 15. show

_____ 16. room

_____ 17. toy

_____ 18. shout

_____ 19. grew

_____ 20. gown

Short vowel sounds
a   e   i   o   u

Blends and digraphs
sp   ch   sh   gr   -ft   -ck

Long vowels
i-e   a-e   ai   oa   ee   ow

Other vowels
oo   oy   ou   ew   ow

score _____/20

_____ 1. crest

_____ 2. hatch

_____ 3. crunch

_____ 4. stripe

_____ 5. grain

_____ 6. chart

_____ 7. spurt

_____ 8. spoil

_____ 9. threw

_____ 10. crawl

_____ 11. dropped

_____ 12. hoping

_____ 13. pickle

_____ 14. shower

_____ 15. groomed

_____ 16. traction

_____ 17. kindly

_____ 18. berries

_____ 19. respectful

_____ 20. reversal

Short vowel sounds
a   e   i   o   u

Blends and digraphs
cr   str   sp   thr   gr   sh
ch   dr   tr
-nch   -st   -tch   -ck

Vowels
i-e   ai   ar   ur   oi
ew   aw   ow   oo   er

Spelling patterns
double consonant
drop final e when adding -ing
change y to i
-le   -tion   -ful   -ly

score _____/20

5. Analyze the results. Record the letter combinations and spelling patterns they represented correctly. Look to see how students handle initial and final consonants and combinations, short and long vowels, and other vowel patterns. Can they hear sounds in order? Did specific words and letter sounds pose difficulty? Look to see if their incorrect spellings use letter combinations that represent sounds in the target word. For example, the vowel sound in *grew* can also be spelled *oo*, but never *oi*.

NAMES TEST

A third source of information comes from having students decode unfamiliar words. Many popular assessments of this kind use a list of nonsense words so that children's sight word knowledge does not interfere with an assessment of their decoding skills. Since I continually work with my students to ensure that they are monitoring for meaning, I am uncomfortable with assessments of this type. Asking them to read nonsense words seems to directly conflict with my goal, that their reading make sense. A good alternative is an adaptation of Patricia Cunningham's Names Test (Cunningham, 1990), shown on page 56, which contains many names present in students' listening vocabularies that are unfamiliar to them in print. Reading names provides a context and purpose for reading isolated words. I have adapted Cunningham's test to be a little shorter and to include a few phonics patterns not included in her original list. You may want to revise the names to reflect particular spelling and/or phonics patterns you want your students to master.

Procedure

1. Make a copy of page 56 for scoring. Either make another copy for students and fold it back so that only the list of names is showing or type the names into a new document and print it out.

2. Administer the test to one student at a time. Explain to the student that he or she will pretend to be a teacher and read the list of names as if they were students in the class. Let the child know that you will not help with any names.

3. Have the student read the entire list.

What About DIBELS?

DIBELS, or Dynamic Indicators of Basic Early Literacy Skills, is widely used across the United States at this time. Many states have made the use of DIBELS a requirement under their Reading First grants as a way of assessing phonemic awareness, phonics, and reading fluency skills. The program, developed by Roland Good and Ruth Kaminski, is described as a tool for predicting students' future performance on standardized tests. However, the focus on students' abilities to generate letter names and letter sounds, and to read nonsense words in a timed setting, does not give me the information that I want. It does not resemble any authentic reading task. As a small part of a more complete assessment package, DIBELS may be useful in some cases, but it does not help me design my instruction. I need assessments that more closely reflect the tasks students face while reading for meaning.

ADAPTED NAMES TEST

Name _____ Date _____ Score _____/40

Tim Hoke   _____ _____

Chuck Cornell   _____ _____

Robin Slade   _____ _____

Patrick Tweed   _____ _____

Gus Quincy   _____ _____

Stanley Shaw   _____ _____

Fred Sherwood   _____ _____

Joan Conway   _____ _____

Jay Clark   _____ _____

Kimberly Blake   _____ _____

Ginger Crowling   _____ _____

Curtis Pointer   _____ _____

Shirley Swain   _____ _____

Flo Thornton   _____ _____

Dee Skidmore   _____ _____

Grace Brewster   _____ _____

Wayne Westmoreland _____ _____

Troy Whitlock   _____ _____

Brice Middleton   _____ _____

June Shackfield   _____ _____

Behaviors noted:

____ sounds letters individually

____ breaks word into syllable parts

____ appeals for help

____ has difficulty with

    consonant blends

    vowel combinations

        final e ay ai

        ee oa oo ow ew

        er ar or ur

        aw oi oy ie

    endings

____ other

Based on "The Names Test" by P. M. Cunningham, 1990, in *The Reading Teacher*, 44, 2.

4. Write a check mark on the answer sheet for each name the student reads correctly. Count first and last names separately. Write phonetic misspellings for misread names.

5. Count a word correct if all the syllables are pronounced correctly, regardless of where the student places the emphasis. With words for which the vowel pronunciation depends on where the syllable is divided, count either pronunciation correct.

6. Score and analyze the results. Look for particular spelling patterns, letter groups, or vowel sounds that are difficult for each student.

SAMPLE PHONICS ASSESSMENT ANALYSIS

These two tests (Spelling Inventory and Adapted Names Test) given in conjunction can give us more complete information about students' phonics knowledge. Let's examine the assessment results of a fourth grader named Tim. His spelling inventory, below, showed he generally understood short vowel sounds, but he had quite a few difficulties representing other vowel sounds appropriately. For example, Tim incorrectly used a final *e* for the short-*a* word *hatch*, and misspelled the long-vowel word *grain*. Tim also had difficulty with *r*-controlled vowels. For example, he spelled *chart* substituting

Intermediate Grades
Spelling Inventory

+ 1. crest
___ 2. hatch *hache*
± 3. crunch
± 4. stripe
___ 5. grain *gran*

___ 6. chart *chort*
___ 7. spurt *spert*
± 8. spoil
___ 9. threw *throw*
___ 10. crawl *crol*

___ 11. dropped *dropt*
± 12. hoping
± 13. pickle
___ 14. shower *shawer*
___ 15. groomed *gromed*

___ 16. traction *tracin*
+ 17. kindly
+ 18. berries
+ 19. respectful
+ 20. reversal

score _10_ /20

Fourth grader Tim's spelling inventory results.

ar with *or*, a letter combination that doesn't represent the same sound. Although he spelled *spurt* incorrectly, the choice of *er* for the vowel sound made sense, since *er* is also used to represent that sound. Tim also had trouble with words with *aw, ew,* and *ow.*

When we compare the names test data below, some similar patterns develop. Tim had difficulty reading words with *aw* and *ew,* as well as *ai, oa, ie, ur,* and *or.* He inconsistently used the sound /s/ to represent *c* when reading. Tim tried to break words into syllables as he began the test, but the longer names toward the end seemed to overwhelm him, and he could no longer successfully work out the individual word parts. He was able to spell the last few multisyllabic words correctly, so it seemed he understood the task and could use it in writing.

The errors Tim made on these assessments indicate that he needs instruction in phonics. I would include Tim in lessons for the vowel patterns he had difficulties with, and also teach him strategies for more consistently breaking words into syllables when reading.

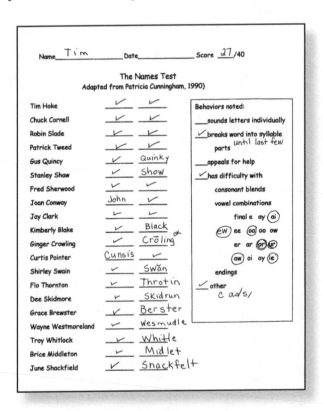

Tim's Names Test results

The rest of this chapter includes a chart to help you determine what phonemic awareness and phonics instructional activities may help your students, followed by descriptions of the activities.

PLAN

Examine the phonemic awareness assessments and the phonics assessments you have administered to your students. Then check this chart to see what strategies or activities may be helpful. Each of these instructional options are explained following this chart.

If the child . . .	Then you might try . . .	Page number
has difficulty identifying individual words in sentences	Be the Sentence Count the Words	61 60
has difficulty identifying syllables in words	Picture Sorts Clap Our Names	64 61
has difficulty hearing and identifying rhymes	Songs, Rhymes, and Stories	63
struggles with segmenting sounds	Elkonin Boxing	67
struggles to blend sounds together	I Say It Slow, You Say It Fast	62
has a meager knowledge of letter names	Alphabet Charts	65
has a meager knowledge of letter sounds	Alphabet Charts/Actions What Word?	65, 66 67
has difficulty hearing vowel sounds	Elkonin Boxing Using Word Chunks	67 70
does not decode words with specific letter combinations	Using Word Chunks T-Chart Words I Know Word Sorts Making Words	70 74 78 76
struggles to decode multisyllable words	I Say It Slow, You Say It Fast Break It Apart Using Word Chunks/Chunk Chart	62 75 70, 72

Phonemic Awareness Activities

The following activities are especially designed to teach phonemic awareness. Many of the activities can also be connected with printed letters to teach phonics at the same time. For example, you can display the printed sentence while you say it when playing Count the Words. The visual example will help students to see and hear word boundaries at the same time. Remember that the research review by the National Reading Panel suggests that we not wait to introduce phonics lessons until students have mastered every aspect of phonemic awareness. Use your judgment, however. For those students struggling the most, it can be confusing to have too many new items included in a lesson. For them, I try to be sure to work orally before I introduce too many written letters.

Some of the beginning phonemic awareness activities, including Picture Sorts, I Say It Slow, You Say It Fast, and Elkonin Boxing, are easily adapted for use with older students who still struggle with phonemic awareness in more complicated words. The adaptations are explained in each section.

COUNT THE WORDS (Large or small group, individual)

Before students can isolate individual sounds, they must be able to find word boundaries. For this activity, each student needs a cup and a set of 10 counters.

● Begin by counting some sets of objects in the room, such as pencils.

● Ask students to drop a counter in the cup for each item as you point to it. Take the counters out of the cup for each new set.

● Then explain that we can also count words the same way. Say a sentence in the normal way, and then repeat the sentence with a pause after each word. As you pause, the students drop a counter into their cup for each word. For example, "Sam likes to play on the slide" would get seven counters.

● Once children can do this, ask them to listen to a new sentence, and then repeat the sentence with you, dropping one counter into the bowl for each word.

- Words with two syllables can be very tricky for some students, since they sometimes think that each syllable makes a word. If you see that students are confusing syllables and words, it's helpful to stop and ask students to listen to see if the individual syllables are real words. As you begin this activity with your students, avoid compound words in your sentences, since it's difficult to tell if a compound word is one word or two when it is spoken.

BE THE SENTENCE (Large or small group)

This is another fun way to help children hear individual words. For this activity, you write each word of a familiar line from a poem or story you've used in shared reading on a separate card. For example, you might choose "Jack and Jill went up the hill."

- Pass out the word cards and ask the children to come up to the front of the room.

- The children can either arrange themselves in order, by matching their position in line to the order of the words on the chart or in the book you used in shared reading, or you can help them get in the correct order.

- Then the children show their cards and say their word to create the sentence. If you use pocket chart poems with your students, you can just take a line of cards at a time out of your pocket chart.

- After each line is created, ask students to count the words.

CLAP OUR NAMES (Large or small group, individual)

Once children can automatically separate sentences into words, they are ready to begin thinking about syllables. Clapping is an effective way to hear these word parts.

- Begin by saying the first name of one child. Say the name again, and clap for each syllable.

- Continue saying names and clapping the syllables. I sometimes call the syllables beats, an easy-to-understand term that seems to go well with the claps.

- Showing students the names you are working with in print enables them to see that words with more beats are usually longer than words with just one beat. Another useful tool that also serves as an interdisciplinary connection is to have the children write their names on graph paper, with one letter in each box, and sort the names by number of syllables.

• When students are able to hear the beats in names, reinforce this throughout the day. For example, you might say, "Everyone with this number of beats in their name can line up now," and clap twice.

I SAY IT SLOW, YOU SAY IT FAST
(Large or small group, individual)

Blending sounds together is a prerequisite skill for being able to decode words—and one that is very difficult for some readers. Oral practice in blending sounds to form words will help students become stronger readers. Some teachers like to introduce this activity with a reading of "Humpty Dumpty." They tell students that these spoken words are broken and need to be put back together again, just like Humpty Dumpty. Other teachers use a turtle puppet that always "talks slow," to say the word parts.

Blending Syllables

• Say the syllables of each word in a list of familiar words with two or three syllables. Have students say the word back to you. You might ask, "Who's name is this? /Sa/ . . . /man/. . . /tha/? That's right, Samantha."

• If you are using other words of more than three syllables, it's helpful to have some pictures for students to choose from, or you can say, "This is a big fruit. /Wat/. . . /er/ . . . /mel/. . . /on/." Keep in mind that sequences of more than three syllables are challenging for young children.

• For older students who are struggling to decode long, multisyllabic words, I select content area words, such as *transportation* and *proclamation*. I don't provide pictures or limit the number of syllables, but I still might suggest that the word is from our social studies unit or give the students some other clue. This particular activity is also a good lead-in to teaching the use of word chunks, as discussed later in this chapter.

Onsets and Rimes

After your students are successful with syllables, move to onsets and rimes. The onset is the beginning consonant or consonant cluster sound that precedes the vowel, and the rime is the vowel and any consonants that follow. For example, the onset of *slip* is /sl/ and the rime is /ip/.

- Say the target words, dividing them into onsets and rimes, and let students tell you the word. (Note: Each syllable in a word generally has an onset and rime, although words or syllables that begin with vowels, like *in* or *am*, do not have an onset. For this activity, choose words with onsets.) You might ask, "Who is this? /Tr/ . . . /avis/. That's right, Travis!"

Phonemes

Finally, you will move into separate phonemes. Phonemes are the smallest unit of speech sounds. They are the individual sounds that make up the word. For example, *slip* has four phonemes, /s/-/l/-/i/-/p/, and lip has only three, /l/-/i/-/p/.

- Say the target words, dividing them into phonemes, and let students tell you the word. Give a context clue to help them. You might say, "I'll say this animal slow, you say it fast, /m/. . . /ou/. . . /s/. That's right, *mouse.*"

When playing this game, select your words with care. Fewer phonemes in a word make the game easier. More than five becomes very difficult. Start with words that have continuant sounds, or those that can be vocalized and elongated. An example like *most* is better to begin with than *got*, since it is easier to exaggerate the sounds in the word *most (mmmmm . . . ooooo . . . ssssss . . . t)* than the sounds of *got*, which often results in the addition of an extra sound to the beginning, like this: /guh/. As children become more attuned to the individual sounds, you will not need to exaggerate the sounds. For students who continue to struggle, choose shorter words with continuant sounds until they are successful.

> When you first introduce an activity that requires students to listen to and blend sounds, use words with **continuant sounds**. These are sounds that can be vocalized and elongated, such as /f/, /l/, /m/, /n/, /r/, /s/, /v/, /w/, /y/, /z/, /th/, /sh/, and vowel sounds.

SONGS, RHYMES, AND STORIES
(Large or small group, individual)

Before they come to school, many children develop phonemic awareness through stories, rhymes, and songs they've heard at home. These items also have an important place in school. Old favorites like nursery rhymes, Dr. Seuss books, and songs like "Down by the Bay" and "The Name Song (Banana Fana Fo Fana)" offer practice with rhymes and phoneme manipulation in a playful context. Many creative teachers have taken old familiar songs and given them a twist to more purposefully teach phonemic awareness, as Hallie Kay Yopp and Ruth Helen Young have demonstrated (2003). "If You're Happy and You Know It" can be transformed into "If You Think You Know This Word" with segmentation and blending of words like this:

There are numerous commercial books and CDs available to provide ready-made songs, rhymes, and activities to support your phonemic awareness instruction. Listed at left are some of my favorites.

Resources for Phonemic Awareness Songs and Activities

Fee, Fie, Phonemic Awareness Activities for Preschoolers by M. Hohmann (Scope Press)

Spring Phonemic Songs and Rhymes by K. Jordano, K. Johnson, & D. Tom (Creative Teaching Press)

Oo-pples and Boo-noo-noos: Songs and Activities for Phonemic Awareness by H. K. Yopp & R. H. Young (Harcourt Brace)

Phonemic Awareness Activities for Early Reading Success by W. Blevins (Scholastic)

Research-Based Reading Lessons for K—3: Phonemic Awareness, Phonics, Fluency, Vocabulary, and Comprehension by M. McLaughlin & L. Fisher (Scholastic)

Sing to Learn (CD) by J. Feldman (www.drjean.org)

PICTURE SORTS
(Large or small group, individual)

Picture sorting is an effective strategy that helps children practice many different elements of phonemic awareness. Introduce this as an independent activity once students can hear the number of beats in words.

● Take individual photos of each child. Write the number of syllables on the back of each picture, so students can check their accuracy.

● Let children sort these pictures by the number of beats in each name. Use a mat divided into numbered columns.

● You might also find pictures of other items to sort by the number of syllables, depending on what you are studying in your class. For example, you might use pictures of farm animals or modes of transportation. Computer clip art or old magazines and workbooks are great sources for pictures.

● Observe your students as they work with these pictures to informally assess their abilities to hear syllables in words.

● When students have begun working with beginning, ending, and middle sounds, picture sorts can be adapted to focus on these areas. You might, for example, provide students with 12 to 15 pictures of items that begin with three different sounds. Students look at all the pictures and group those that sound the same.

As you begin this type of activity, keep in mind two things. First, be sure that children understand what the pictures represent. Be open to different interpretations of pictures. If you've included a picture of a *man*, but your student puts it in the group with *bear*, ask for an explanation. The student might have considered the picture a *boy*. Second, begin with distinct sounds, such as /m/ and /s/. Save tasks that require discrimination between similar sounds, such as /b/ and /p/, for later, when your students are better able to hear the differences. Remember also that English language learners may have great difficulty discriminating sounds that are not used in their native languages. You may need to keep those sounds out of the tasks at first.

ALPHABET CHARTS (Large or small group, individual)

Alphabet charts give students a key word to use as a reference for letters and their representative sounds. It is important for some struggling readers that the same alphabet chart be used wherever they read. Therefore, it is good to have a common chart across the school—for example, in the reading specialist's room, the first-grade class, and the speech teacher's room.

It's also important that students understand exactly what the picture represents. Check to see what is causing confusion. One of my students spent several days thinking that *n* represented the sound heard at the beginning of *eggs*, since the nest pictured with *n* had eggs in it. The picture of *elephant*, which often represents *e*, can also cause confusion, since many children hear the letter name *l* at the beginning of *elephant*. For students with a meager vocabulary, it is well worth your time to make an individual alphabet chart using pictures that represent words from such students' speaking vocabulary. I usually cut several pictures from magazines, old reading workbooks, or other sources, and let the student choose a picture he or she knows and wants. You can also discuss words with a particular beginning sound, and search for or draw a picture to represent a word the student likes. While individual alphabet charts conflict with the idea of having common charts throughout the school, it is worth it for your most struggling students to have a set of self-selected picture cues. For them, if a great deal of mental effort goes into trying to remember the name of the class chart picture, it is not useful as a quick reference.

You will get the most value from an alphabet chart if you use it with the students on a regular basis. I like to start my kindergarten and beginning first-grade reading lessons by chanting the chart with my students. At first, I point to the letters and the pictures, but as the days go by we all take a turn as the pointer. As I point to the uppercase letter, the lowercase letter,

and the picture, we chant like this: "A, a, apple /a/, /a/, /a/. B, b, ball /b/, /b/, /b/."
Sometimes we start with a different letter or go backwards from *z*. It's a daily
routine. I also like children to have matching individual alphabet charts, so
they can all point as we move through the letters, pictures, and sounds.

ALPHABET ACTIONS (Large or small group, individual)

To encourage learning, we try to use as many modalities as we can. Assigning
actions that begin with the sound of each letter can be an effective way to help
students struggling to remember letter sounds. As you and your children recite the
alphabet, say the action and act it out together. Once children have learned actions
for many of the letters, I like to practice whenever we need a little movement break.

- Have students stand up. As you show them a letter, either from a card or
  written on the board, have them do the appropriate action until you hide or
  erase the letter.

- Alternately, you can also pass out magnetic letters to individual children and
  let each child get up and do the required action. The child can call on someone to guess which letter he or she acted out.

This activity lends itself to making a fun class book, with one letter on each page
accompanied by digital photos of your students doing the action. The book
can then be used during shared reading to review and act out the actions. See the
alphabet actions I've suggested below, or develop your own with your students.

Alphabet Actions

A Act (extend arms in dramatic fashion)

B Bounce (pretend to bounce ball)

C Catch (pretend to catch a ball)

D Dive (hold arms in diving position)

E Enter (pretend to come through a door)

F Fly (flap arms as if flying)

G Give (pretend to give a gift)

H Hop (hop on one foot or make your fingers hop)

I Itch (scratch self)

J Jog (jog in place)

K Kiss (kiss in the air and hug self)

L Laugh (pretend to laugh)

M March (march in place)

N Nap (lay head on hands as if going to sleep)

O Open (open eyes wide)

P Push (extend arms and push)

Q Quiet (put finger on lips)

R Roll (roll hands)

S Stretch (stretch arms wide)

T Tickle (wiggle fingers)

U Up (point up with thumb)

V Vibrate (jiggle all over)

W Wonder (tap head and look puzzled)

X X-ray (pretend to x-ray hand)

Y Yawn (pretend to yawn)

Z Zoom (move hand quickly)

WHAT WORD? (Large or small group, individual)

This activity is great for helping students isolate beginning sounds. It is effective because it uses familiar pictures, which narrows the possibilities and helps them focus on the sounds. It also is useful for developing memory of the sound represented by each letter. To use this activity, you need a large alphabet chart (see page 65) displayed in a spot that is visible to all of your students, or individual copies of the chart. Explain to the children that you are going to get ready to say one of the pictures on the chart. Their job is to figure out which picture you are going to say. It goes like this, "What word am I getting ready to say? /m/ . . . That's right! *Monkey* begins with /m/."

When you do this activity, be careful with letters like *p* and *t*. Don't articulate an extra sound, like "puh" for /p/. Be sure to make just the sound. After you've modeled this activity several times, let students have a turn saying the first sound.

ELKONIN BOXING AND SHARED AND GUIDED WRITING (Large or small group, individual)

Shared, or interactive, writing is an excellent vehicle for working with sounds and letters. During shared writing, students and teacher work together to develop and physically write a message. Many teachers write a morning message with students each day as an authentic purpose for writing. Other opportunities for authentic writing arise throughout the day, for example, during science as you record observations made during an experiment. Using Elkonin boxes during shared writing will help students successfully stretch words, and listen for and represent sounds in the context of the writing. It builds on sound-symbol relationships students know, and gives a context for teaching new ones.

Elkonin boxing (or sound boxing) is a tool used in Marie Clay's (2005) literacy lessons that transfers very well into general classroom instruction. Each phoneme of a word is represented by an individual box. Thus, the word *dog* would have three boxes, and the word *chick* would also have three boxes, since both the *ch* and the *ck* are examples of two letters working together to make one sound.

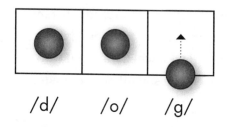

/d/   /o/   /g/

In Elkonin boxing, children move a counter into the box as they say each sound.

When you first introduce Elkonin boxes, you will want to work in small groups of no more than four students. You will need counters, and a set of boxes drawn on paper or small whiteboards for each child.

● Draw the same number of boxes as there are sounds in the words you will say. You may decide to use pictures to represent the words. I find it easiest to begin with words with only two sounds, such as *key*, *me*, or *go*.

● At first, the children push one counter for each sound into the boxes as they segment the word orally. For example, with *go* they would say /g/ and /o/ as they push the counters into the appropriate boxes. This can be difficult for some children at first, since they have several things to think about simultaneously: the sounds, saying the sounds, and pushing the counter. It can be hard to push the counter and make the sound at the same time.

● After students can segment the sounds in the word, ask them how they can write what they hear. Don't be surprised if they respond with the final sound before they tell you the other sounds. It's a common response, and nothing to be worried about. Go ahead and let them record the sound with the letter that represents the sound or write it for them if they are unable to form the letter. Prompt as necessary with questions like:

> *What else can you hear?*
>
> *What can you hear at the beginning?*

● Fill in the letters for any parts of the word the children do not know. This is a great opportunity to introduce some sound-symbol relationships that the students have not yet learned, but don't try to teach too many things at once. When you choose the words for this activity, keep in mind what sounds your students can already represent, and try to provide opportunities to practice these sounds along with learning some new sound-symbol relationships.

● As children become more adept at segmenting the words, it is no longer necessary to use the counters. Encourage the children to point at the boxes as they say the individual sounds, and then fill in the letters to represent the sounds. If students use incorrect letters, simply cover up or erase the mistake and write the correct letter for them. I think it's important to validate what students did well when they make an attempt, especially if the error is caused by the sometimes confusing spelling patterns of English. For example, if they write the letter *c* as the beginning of *kitten*, I might say, "You know that the letter *c* can represent the sound you hear at the beginning, but this word starts with another letter that represents the same sound, *k*."

Once students understand Elkonin boxes, we use them to segment and represent sounds in words during shared writing lessons. I keep a whiteboard with me, and as we encounter unfamiliar words, I draw the boxes for the sounds on the board, and ask, "What do you hear in this word? How should I write it? Show me where to put it." You may also want students to have individual boards to figure out the words with you.

Elkonin Boxes in Guided Writing

In guided writing lessons for beginning readers in kindergarten and first grade, I gather a small, homogeneous group of four or five students. Students will need paper and a pencil or markers. You may also use cover-up tape or computer labels to fix errors. My students have individual writing books made by binding about 20 sheets of unlined paper together.

- To begin, we come up with a short story of one or two sentences that we will all write. First we count the words, and I write lines on their papers for each word. As students become more capable, I stop drawing the lines for them.

- We repeat the story, and point to each line as we say the words.

- Then we begin writing. For any words students do not automatically know, we use Elkonin boxes to figure them out. In their work space, the left-hand page of my students' writing books, I quickly draw the number of boxes necessary for the word.

- Students work independently or with my help to write the sounds they can represent with letters. Then they transfer the word into their story and keep writing.

While Elkonin boxes are used extensively with beginning readers, they also can be useful for older struggling readers who are having difficulty hearing the individual sounds in words. Laurice M. Joseph (1998) used the boxes with learning-disabled students in second, third, and fourth grade, and found that the students' word identification and spelling skills improved.

Designing Phonemic Awareness Lessons

When designing phonemic awareness lessons, use these guidelines.

- Keep it short—no more than 15 minutes for a lesson.

- Keep it fun and playful.

- Keep it meaningful. Select words from texts you are using in the classroom, or use student names.

- Keep it sequential. Don't expect students to be able to manipulate phonemes if they can't identify the sounds in words.

- Remember that the purpose of phonemic awareness is to enable students to use letters to read and spell. Instruction in reading and writing words and sentences often enables students to make progress with phonemic awareness tasks as well. Don't wait until all tasks are mastered to begin reading instruction.

Phonics Activities

The following activities are excellent for helping students learn phonics patterns, which help them decode unfamiliar words.

USING WORD CHUNKS
(Large or small group, individual)

While vowels can represent many different sounds, certain combinations of vowels and consonants are almost always pronounced the same, such as the combination -*all*. These spelling patterns have been called word families, rimes, and phonograms, but I prefer the term "chunk." Whatever you call them, they are a useful tool for decoding unknown words. In fact, Edward Fry found that the 38 most common chunks (see page 72) can be used to spell more than 650 common one-syllable words (Fry, 1998). The chunks are useful in moving children away from slow, letter-by-letter decoding, and are particularly useful for older students when decoding multisyllabic words. Trying to decode long words letter by letter is too difficult, since it is hard to remember more than five or six individual phonemes long enough to blend them into a word.

The Role of Phonics "Rules"

For generations of students, teachers have used general rules to give students tools for decoding unknown words. Catchy terms and phrases, such as "magic e," "bossy r," and "When two vowels go walking, the first one does the talking," have been coined to help students understand and be able to apply a specific rule of spelling. But just how helpful are some of those tried-and-true rules? Theodore Clymer did an interesting study back in 1963 to investigate the usefulness of 45 of the most common rules when applied to 2,600 words students generally see in the primary grades.

Clymer examined four basic reading series plus the words from the Gates Reading Vocabulary for the Primary Grades. His findings were fascinating. Many of these so-called rules aren't actually true most of the time. Clymer found that only 18 rules worked in at least 75 percent of the words, and many involved consonant clusters such as *ch, ck,* and *gh,* or accenting rules for syllables. The rules for vowels were much tougher. In fact, he found that when two vowels are side by side ("walking"), the long sound of the first one is heard and the second is silent in only 45 percent of the words he examined. It works for *rain, boat,* and *meat,* but not for *said, friend,* or *great.* His research also showed that when there are two vowels, one of which is a final ("magic") *e,* the first vowel is long and the *e* is silent in only 63 percent of common primary grade vocabulary. So the magic *e* and talking vowels don't seem to be a good gamble for students. The odds are against them being able to solve the words using these devices.

Another problem with rules is how easily students confuse them. Students have confidently explained to me that when there is an *l* or *p* or *m* (or about any other letter they happen on) following a vowel, it reaches over and makes the letter say its own name. As you can see, children take a fragment of something they've heard before (in this case, "two vowels walking") and try to make it work for a word they are trying to decode, with often poor results.

Common "Chunks"

Here, the most common chunks are listed in order of the frequency with which they appear in single-syllable words.

Rank	Chunk	Example	Rank	Chunk	Example
1.	-ay	day	20.	-ug	bug
2.	-ill	hill	21.	-op	hop
3.	-ip	lip	22.	-in	chin
4.	-at	cat	23.	-an	man
5.	-am	ham	24.	-est	nest
6.	-ag	bag	25.	-ink	pink
7.	-ack	pack	26.	-ow	snow
8.	-ank	bank	27.	-ew	chew
9.	-ick	chick	28.	-ore	store
10.	-ell	bell	29.	-ed	red
11.	-ot	pot	30.	-ab	crab
12.	-ing	ring	31.	-ob	job
13.	-ap	cap	32.	-ock	clock
14.	-unk	junk	33.	-ake	cake
15.	-ail	nail	34.	-ine	line
16.	-ain	rain	35.	-ight	night
17.	-eed	seed	36.	-im	swim
18.	-y	fly	37.	-uck	duck
19.	-out	shout	38.	-um	gum

From Edward Fry, 1998

Before you begin to teach these chunks, remember that some letter patterns may represent more than one sound. For example, *ow* represents the long *o* sound, as in *blow*, as well as the sound heard in *cow*. Keep in mind that readers must be flexible when using word chunks. Don't hide the exceptions.

To begin teaching students to use chunks, select a word they already know that contains the chunk, perhaps from a text they've read. Gather children around so they can see, and make your key word with magnetic letters. I introduce the lesson like this:

> "Boys and girls, today I am going to show you how knowing just this one word can help you to figure out many other words. This skill will help you when you read for the rest of your life! Are you ready?
>
> Here is a word you know. [I display the word using magnetic letters.] That's right. It's your name, isn't it, Jack?
>
> Now watch me carefully. I'm going to pull off the *J* in Jack's name. What does this part represent? [I point to the letter *j*.] That's right, this letter represents the sound /j/. And this part of the word represents the sound /ack/. Let me put it back together. *Jack*. Make the sound of its parts when I pull it apart: /j/ . . . /ack/. Put it back together. *Jack*.
>
> Now look what I'm doing. [I build the word *sack* right below *Jack*, using magnetic letters.] What do you notice about this word? That's right, it has the same letters as the end of *Jack*. Often those letters represent the same sounds, and they can help you figure out this new word.
>
> The *s* represents the sound /s/ and the *ack* represents /ack/. If we put it together we get *sack*! A sack is like a bag. We're going to read a book today about a balloon that keeps saying 'Go jump in a sack!'
>
> [I mix up the letters for the word *sack*.] Who can use the word *Jack* to help them build the word *sack*? [I give the letters to a student and let her build the word right below *Jack*.] Let's read both words: *Jack*, *sack*!
>
> Now I'm going to put this word up on this chart, along with Jack's picture, so we remember that it's his name. I will put it in this section, under the *a*, and I'm going to highlight the letters *ack*, so we can easily spot them. This chart will be filled with chunks, or pieces of words, that can help us figure out new words."

Many of the words you might have on your classroom word wall (see Chapter 3, page 98) contain useful chunks, for example, *went* or *right*. Other good sources are the names of the children in your classroom or familiar brand names, such as *Tide*.

Notice in the lesson above I did not make a whole list of words that rhyme with *Jack*. Rather than teaching a bunch of words, I was showing students how words work, and the strategy of using a word they know to figure out a word they don't know, by using analogy.

The next day, I would repeat the lesson, using a very different key word, for example, the word *hill*.

A chunk chart in progress for the primary grades. Notice the picture accompanying each word and the highlighted chunk.

T-CHART WORDS I KNOW (Large or small group, individual)

In order to give students practice combining their knowledge of phonics with meaning clues to cross-check for accuracy, I like to use T-Charts. Patricia Cunningham (1995) developed this activity and described it in *Phonics They Use* as "Using Words You Know." I've adapted it slightly to use a T-Chart.

● In preparation, use sentence strips to write eight to ten sentences that use words with two target chunks from your chunk chart (above). For example, you may want to practice *-ack* and *-ill*. You would write sentences containing words like *shack*, *pack*, *fill*, and *spill*.

● Fold the strips so only the words with the chunks show.

● Select the two key words listed on your chunk chart (e.g., *Jack* and *hill*). Ask students to create a T-Chart on their paper and write one key word at the top of each column. Ask them to underline the chunks in both words.

- Next, show them a word from the sentence strips. Ask them to write it in the column under the key word with the same chunk, and use the chunk to decode the new word. Say something like, "If *J-a-c-k* is *Jack*, *s-h-a-c-k* must be *shack*."

- Reveal the sentence and check to see that the word the students decoded makes sense in the sentence. *The man lived in an old shack in the woods.*

- Repeat with the other sentences. End the lesson by asking students to read the key words and all the new words they've written on their T-Chart.

- The next time, choose two new words and chunks to create a new T-Chart.

Jack	hill
shack	mill
black	spill
	fill

shack

The man lived in an old : shack : in the woods.

After doing this lesson with two words a few times, ask the students to begin with three key words and chunks. Continue adding key words (and columns to your chart) in subsequent lessons until students are comparing six or more chunks to select the appropriate word they know. At first, use very different spelling patterns, like *hill* and *Jack*, but as students become more adept, choose chunks that are more visually similar, such as *-ew*, *-ow*, and *-er*.

BREAK IT APART (Large or small group, individual)

Chunks are useful for older students as well. I teach my older students to follow a routine for decoding big words. When they find a word they can't figure out using other means, they write it down on paper or a whiteboard and begin their analysis.

- First, they look for prefixes, suffixes, and endings (see Chapter 3 for information on teaching these) and circle any that they know.

- Then they underline all the vowels and check for chunks or spelling patterns that they know.

- Last, they blend the chunks together with the surrounding letters to try to make a word that makes sense in the sentence. For example, if the word in the sentence is *marshmallows*, they might make the following connections:

> *marshmallows: ar as in car, all as in fall, ow as in blow*
> Marsh . . . mall . . . ows. Marshmallows!
> *Jason put a big bag of marshmallows in his pack.*

(Although the *all* is not pronounced the same way as in *all*, it is close enough to make pronouncing the word possible, especially once the context of the sentence is taken into consideration.)

To teach this routine, model decoding big words using these same steps whenever you are reading aloud to your students. The routine takes practice and support, just like any other strategy.

MAKING WORDS (Large or small group, individual)

Making Words is an active, hands-on activity developed by Patricia Cunningham (1995). It provides an excellent format for helping students learn how spelling patterns work and how changing the letters or the order of letters in a word changes the whole word. Like T-Chart Words I Know, this activity uses phonics by analogy, with children using words they know to spell and read other words with the same patterns.

Although this activity can be used with a whole class, I find I am able to monitor student responses and adjust my teaching far better in groups no larger than eight. Each child needs a set of letters to manipulate—either plastic magnetic letters or a set written on individual 2- by 2-inch cards. You will also need target words written on 5- by 8-inch index cards and a pocket chart.

Select the target words your students will make. First, choose two or three spelling patterns you want to focus on. I usually use previously introduced patterns from the chunk wall. In your first lessons, you will want your chunks to be quite different, but as students learn more about how spelling patterns work, you may want to have patterns that differ by fewer letters, for example, *-ick* ,*-ike*, and *-ink*.

Make a list of four or five words for each chunk. I like to include some words with the same onset, but different rimes, such as *lick*, *like*, and *link*. Include some words that contain the same letters but do not follow the patterns, such as *in*, *is*, and *let*. Sort your words from smallest to largest, and arrange them in an order that allows children to see that when you change or add a letter, the word changes in a predictable way.

In Cunningham's lessons, the letters are all combined to make one large word at the end of the lesson. I generally do not select my words in this way, since I do not want to be limited in the letters I can use in my lesson. If you do opt to have a secret word for students to build at the end, you may want to select a word from a text students are reading, or a content area theme.

In that case, check the letters of the word for possible letter-sound patterns you can focus on and then list your words.

Here's how a lesson focusing on short vowel *e, -ink, -ick*, and *–ike* might work.

● Write these words on index cards ahead of time: *in, it, sit, set, ten, bet, ink, like, link, lick, hike, sick, sink, bike, bent, sent, nets, stick, licks, likes, links*.

● Give students the letters they need: *e, i, b, c, h, k, l, n, s, t*.

● Tell students, "Take two of your letters and build the word *in*. We are *in* school. Now run your finger under the letters to see if you spelled the word correctly. Say the sounds and check to see if you have *in*."

● Show the word card *in* and ask, "Were you right?" Place the word in the pocket chart.

● "Now change one of your letters to make the word *it*. *It* is Tuesday today. Check that you are right." Show the word card.

● "This time, add one letter to the word *it* to make the new word *sit*. I like to *sit* in the sun."

● For the next word, say, "This time, you need to change one of the letters to a new one. Listen hard to the middle sound and make the word *set*. My job is to *set* the table."

● Continue the lesson the same way, letting students know when to add letters, change letters, or rearrange the letters they have to make a new word (e.g., *sent* and *nets*).

● Once you have built all the words, it's time to sort them, following this procedure:

  1. Ask students to read all the words in the pocket chart with you.

  2. Pick up a word and ask, "Who can find a word that rhymes with _____?"

  3. As the rhyming words are found, place them under the selected word in the pocket chart.

  4. Repeat with the rest of your target chunks.

● After the words are sorted, read them again, and remind students that often thinking of a word they know can help them to read a new word.

● Finally, ask students what word could help them if they were reading and saw these words: *shrink, Mike, quickly*. Which words could help them spell these: *stink, spent, chick*?

When you design Making Words lessons, keep in mind which phonics patterns and chunks your students need practice on. Remember to refer to the assessment data you have collected. For older students, use multisyllabic words that contain the phonics patterns that are difficult for them.

WORD SORTS (Large or small group, individual)

each	rich
reach	witch
beach	switch
teach	hatch
	match
	catch

Word Sorts are like the Picture Sorts described on page 64, but instead of sorting pictures to practice phonemic awareness, students sort word cards to practice phonics. Just as pictures can be sorted in different ways, word cards can be sorted by sound, specific vowel patterns, or common affixes or roots, depending on your instructional purpose. Asking students to create their own group from a given set of words can be a very good informal assessment that reveals specific features of words students attend to. For example, given the following words, some students may sort them into rhymes while others may make groups of words with short and long vowel sounds: *reach, rich, each, teach, beach, witch, switch, hatch, match, catch.* If you select the categories, you can control what aspects of words students focus on. You can also informally evaluate students' decoding skills by examining their sorted cards.

You can control the difficulty of word sorts by making the words more or less similar in structure, sound, or other feature. If you are asking students to sort words by the way they sound, it is important that they be able to read most of the words. However, if you are asking students to use words they know to solve unknown words, you may include some unfamiliar words with the same spelling patterns.

Final Thoughts

Being able to discriminate, manipulate, and use the sounds of our language is crucial to being able to read. Phonics deserves to be taught in your classroom, and taught in a direct and sequential way. Use the assessments at the beginning of the chapter to determine how to place your students into smaller groups to effectively focus on the areas that will accelerate their reading progress. Not everyone in your class will need the same instruction. Remember that phonics is a means to an end. Teaching children how to decode strings of isolated words will not necessarily make them better readers. In the next chapter, we will focus on how to help students understand the meaning of the words they successfully decode.

Resources and Further Reading

Bear, D. R., Invernizzi, M., Templeton, S., & Johnston, F. (2000). *Words their way: Word study for phonics, vocabulary, and spelling instruction.* Upper Saddle River, NJ: Prentice Hall.

Blevins, W. (1997). *Phonemic awareness activities for early reading success.* New York: Scholastic.

Blevins, W. (2001). *Teaching phonics & word study in the intermediate grades.* New York: Scholastic.

Clay, M. (1993). *An observation survey of early literacy achievement.* Portsmouth, NH: Heinemann,

Clay, M. (2005). *Literacy lessons designed for individuals, part two: Teaching procedures.* Portsmouth, NH: Heinemann.

Clymer, T. (1963). The utility of phonic generalizations in the primary grades. *The Reading Teacher, 16,* 252–258.

Cunningham, P. M. (1990). The Names Test: A quick assessment of decoding ability. *The Reading Teacher, 44* (2), pp. 124–129.

Cunningham, P. M. (1995). *Phonics they use* (2nd ed.). New York: Harper Colllins.

Fry, E. (1998). The most common phonograms. *The Reading Teacher, 51,* 620–622.

Goodman, K. S. (2000). *The truth about DIBELS.* Portsmouth, NH: Heinemann.

Hohmann, M. (2002). *Fee, fie, phonemic awareness: 130 activities for preschoolers.* Ypsilanti, MI: High/Scope Press.

Joseph, L. M. (1998). Word boxes help children with learning disabilities identify and spell words. *The Reading Teacher, 52,* 348–356.

McLaughlin, M. & Fisher, L. (2005). *Research-based reading lessons for K–3: Phonemic awareness, phonics, fluency, vocabulary and comprehension.* New York: Scholastic.

Pinnell, G. & Fountas, I. C. (1998). *Word matters.* Portsmouth, NH: Heinemann.

Yopp, H. K. & Young, R. H. (2003). *Oo-pples and boo-noo-noos: Songs and activities for phonemic awareness.* New York: Harcourt Brace.

Chapter 3

Vocabulary

Classroom Snapshot

A group of fifth-grade students were working quietly at their seats on their state's multiple-choice reading test. Although students were aware that they could have no assistance, one boy continued to wave his hand frantically in the air. Finally, unable to stand it any longer, the teacher walked over.

"Tom, what's the problem? You know I can't help you."

"Mrs. White, they keep saying 'in the text.' I don't know what a text is," said the boy.

The above example is an especially sad instance of unfamiliar vocabulary creating a problem with reading comprehension. It happened in my classroom a few years ago. Because my student didn't understand the term *text*, he was unable to answer the questions on the test, and to demonstrate his abilities to read and comprehend.

Inadequate vocabulary knowledge is a problem for many students. They often encounter words they have never seen before, or they rely on known meanings of words without regard to the sentence context, as one of my students did when she explained confidently that "the mother spoke *crossly*" meant she was in the middle of crossing the street. (She wasn't.) Our most struggling readers often have access to such a small number of high-frequency, or sight, words that meaning is consistently disrupted as they painstakingly work their way through a text. In this chapter, we will examine the role of reading vocabulary, sight word vocabulary, and learning strategies for figuring out unfamiliar words. We will look at ways to assess vocabulary knowledge and skills, and how to use the results to plan effective instruction in your classroom.

What Is Reading Vocabulary?

There are different definitions of vocabulary. Researchers distinguish between oral vocabulary and reading vocabulary. Oral vocabulary refers to the words we recognize in speaking and listening. Reading vocabulary means the words we can read and understand. As students read, they decode written text and translate it into oral language. Students with larger oral vocabularies will be able to easily develop larger reading vocabularies. Students who decode words that are not in their oral vocabulary have trouble understanding them. Development of oral vocabulary contributes to the development of reading vocabulary.

Relationship to Other Areas of Reading

Vocabulary is related to phonics ability. A student may be able to apply phonics skills to decode a word, but if the word isn't in his or her speaking vocabulary, it won't help much. Conversely, if your student "knows" a word orally, he or she will find it easier to decode the word and use it to help make sense of the text.

Vocabulary knowledge is a key component of fluency. The more unfamiliar words students encounter in a passage, the longer it takes for them to get through the text as they laboriously figure out each previously unknown word. When too much energy is spent figuring out individual words, students are less likely to think about the way text should sound. Sometimes, to maintain momentum, students simply skip over the unknown words, which diminishes their comprehension of the passage.

Vocabulary knowledge has its biggest impact on comprehension. Quite simply, if a reader doesn't know what most of the words in a text mean, he or she can't understand the text. Perhaps you've forgotten what that feels like, since you have such a broad vocabulary. Try the following paragraph. You will probably be able to pronounce and define every word, but can you understand the words in this context?

> The opening pair were both out for ducks. Inverarity viciously pulled Brown into the gully but was sent retiring to the pavilion by a shooter from Cox. Jones in slips and Chappell at silly mid on were superb, and Daniel bowled a maiden over in his first spell.

(Adapted from Brian Cambourne, *The whole story: Natural learning and the acquisition of literacy in the classroom*. Auckland, New Zealand: Scholastic, 1988, p. 161)

Unless you have some knowledge of cricket, this news article was probably incomprehensible to you. Do you know who is winning? And perhaps more importantly, do you even care? Trying to work through text where many of the words and their meanings are unfamiliar to you is hard going. Many students simply quit trying.

We will focus on two types of vocabulary in this chapter: high-frequency words, including **sight words**, such as *said, could,* and *the,* and more sophisticated words, such as *enormous, disappear,* and *foolish,* which I refer to as **general reading vocabulary**.

Sight word identification is very important for beginning readers. Their early books are filled with sight words. As their name suggests, these words must be known by sight, since they don't follow normal phonics "rules" and they occur frequently. Students must be able to recognize them with ease and automaticity. As one of my kindergarten colleagues puts it, "They must get stuck in your head." Students who have difficulty with sight words will probably read with poor accuracy, fluency, and comprehension.

To add further complexity for young readers, many high-frequency words (both sight words and phonetically regular words that appear frequently in texts), such as *of* and *would,* don't have a clear meaning attached to them. Because students can't access the word meanings, they often mix up these "function words." It astounds many parents that their child can easily read a big word such as *hippopotamus,* but continues to mix up *for* and *of.* Even more advanced readers continue to mix up some of these words, which can have a negative impact on comprehension. For example, a student may read a text as, "She got a cup *of* coffee," rather than "a cup *for* coffee." These function words may not change the meaning of a sentence drastically, but they can cause confusion.

General reading vocabulary words are important for your students' reading success in a different way than sight words are. Such words often are more mature or precise labels for concepts students already understand, such as *commotion, absurd,* and *reluctant.* They may also be descriptions of ideas or concepts that are new, such as *latitude* and *orbit.* These reading vocabulary words are generally more of a problem for older students. At the earliest reading levels, most words students are expected to read are in the students' speaking vocabulary. Beginning reading books contain fewer hard words, and if they are present, the words are often accompanied by a picture to make the meaning clear.

Around second grade, as students become more capable readers, texts generally become more sophisticated, and the reading vocabulary richer. More and more of the words become "story language," or words that are not generally used in spoken conversation. This is when comprehension problems develop.

In an attempt to solve this comprehension problem, the basal reading programs popular in the 1970s used controlled vocabulary lists, and were characterized by taking familiar children's stories and changing the text using words the publishers expected to be in the children's oral language vocabulary and, therefore, understood. For example, Ann McGovern's book *Too Much Noise* was revised for a basal text. The original went like this:

> A long time ago there was an old man. His name
> was Peter, and he lived in an old, old house.
>
> The bed creaked. The floor squeaked. Outside,
> the wind blew the leaves through the trees.
> The leaves fell on the roof. Swish. Swish.
> The tea kettle whistled. Hiss. Hiss.
>
> "Too noisy," said Peter.
>
> (Ann McGovern, *Too Much Noise*, Scholastic, 1967)

The text was adapted for a first-grade reading book as follows:

> Peter was an old man who lived in an old,
> old house.
>
> There was too much noise in Peter's house. The
> bed made noise. The door made noise. And the
> window made noise. Peter didn't like all that noise.
>
> (*A Place for Me*, Holt, Rinehart, and Winston, 1973, pp. 104–105)

The language has been simplified. Descriptive, but perhaps unfamiliar, words like *creaked, squeaked, swish,* and *hiss* have been removed. It's meant to be easier for students to read, but it seems much less interesting, doesn't it?

Simplifying vocabulary in this way is not as prevalent in today's reading texts, which often contain rich and descriptive language. As more and more teachers moved toward using trade books to teach reading in a whole-language approach, publishing literature with controlled vocabulary was no longer possible. Today's basal texts continue to be characterized by authentic literature from trade books, complete with rich language, and words that may be unfamiliar to most students. We can assist students to read these rich texts by teaching some specific vocabulary, but we can't always be there to troubleshoot a text for them.

As children read independently, they will run into unfamiliar words. Teachers cannot teach all of the potential 3,000 unfamiliar words a year students may encounter. So word-learning strategies become essential for students to figure out words on their own. These independent word-learning strategies include using sentence context, referring to visuals such as pictures and diagrams, and structural analysis using word parts (root words and affixes like *un-* and *-ly*) to determine a word's meaning.

How Word-Learning Strategies Work

Here is an example of how we might use word-learning strategies to figure out the term *gynecocracy* in a sophisticated text. The excerpt reads:

Few people live in a gynecocracy.

- The first step in developing word knowledge is monitoring. Students must be able to identify unknown words. Were you able to find the tricky part in the sentence above? The word *gynecocracy* is probably unfamiliar to you.

- Let's apply some word-learning strategies. The context of this sentence suggests that *gynecocracy* is something not many people live in. It could be a strange kind of house, but are you sure?

- Next, we will use structural analysis. Do you recognize some word parts?

  Gyne-, as in *gynecology*
  -ocracy, as in *democracy*

Gynecology has to do with women, and democracy is a kind of government. Could it be a government run by women?

- Did you then check it in the sentence to see if it made sense? It does, doesn't it? I think we've got the meaning of this word.

- Were you ever tempted to jump up and run to the dictionary? I doubt that you were. And even if you had, few dictionaries seem to have this word. For adult readers, dictionaries are a last resort. Yet in the classroom, it's one of the most common strategies taught.

Vocabulary Development

Vocabulary develops in many ways. Students learn some words through independent reading, but some students do very little independent reading, and when they do, they tend to skip over unknown words, so they don't learn many words that way.

Some words are learned through discussions and other experiences with oral language. Home environment plays a large part in oral vocabulary development. Students who have had varied experiences, such as trips to the zoo, gardening, or camping, along with plenty of oral communication and/or book reading at home, have larger oral vocabularies, which transfer easily into reading vocabulary. Students with meager speaking vocabularies will need to learn the meaning of many words orally and then see what they look like in print. Repeated opportunities to talk about children's experiences and the texts they read will be very important for helping these students build strong reading vocabularies.

Researcher Camille Blachowicz (2005) describes an oral and reading vocabulary development program that uses a thematic approach with posters, discussion, words written on sticky notes, and a series of five related books. Students look at large pictures and contribute words suggested by the photo. Teachers write the words on sticky notes on the photo, and provide opportunities to relate the words to one another by sorting the words into many different categories. After listening to content area books with the same theme, students contribute more words to the list. Finally, students are invited to use the words in a written assignment. Blachowicz's work has produced positive vocabulary development results with students from kindergarten through middle school.

Students also learn many words by direct instruction. Selecting certain words from a text and teaching those words to students before reading not only improves comprehension of the specific selection, but boosts general vocabulary learning. But which words should you select?

Beck, McKeown, and Kucan (2002) identify three different tiers of vocabulary words. Tier 1 words are very basic words that almost all students know without instruction, such as *baby, happy,* and *walk.* Many of these words are sight words that the students are working to recognize.

The second tier contains words that are more sophisticated, but still found in many texts across a variety of domains, such as *fortunate, balcony,* and *struggle*. Tier 2 words are well worth direct instruction, as students will see these words in many contexts, but since there are about 7,000 of them, teachers cannot directly teach them all.

Tier 3 words are relatively unusual words that are primarily used in particular subject areas, such as *isotope*. These words are directly taught when they are part of a specific lesson, such as in a science class.

Students also learn words on their own by applying strategies such as word analysis and using content clues to determine meaning.

Finally, students learn many general vocabulary words by simply developing an awareness of words. Activities that encourage students to become aware of and discuss interesting or unknown words they encounter go a long way toward developing general reading vocabulary.

What Does Research Say About Vocabulary?

Students come to school with great variations in their oral vocabularies. As Hart and Risley (1995) reported in *Meaningful Differences in the Everyday Experiences of Young American Children: The Everyday Experience of One- and Two-Year-Old American Children,* young children from advantaged homes (those with well educated parents and high economic status) may have receptive oral vocabularies more than five times as large as children from economically disadvantaged homes (those receiving Aid to Dependent Children). This means that some children in your class may be able to understand five times more words than other children. White, Graves, and Slater (1990) found that the trend continued into elementary school, when they examined students in first through fifth grades. They found that the reading and meaning vocabularies of children in high socioeconomic homes grew more rapidly than those of children from low-income homes.

The National Reading Panel's review of research suggests that vocabulary should be taught both directly and indirectly (NRP, p. 4-24), and other researchers have estimated that children need to learn 3,000 words a year (Baumann, Kame'enui, & Ash, 2003). While we cannot teach each word explicitly, the report recommends that vocabulary instruction be incorporated into reading instruction, particularly vocabulary items that are required for comprehending a specific text. In fact, direct instruction in key vocabulary influences comprehension of specific texts more than any other factor (Nagy, 1988).

It also is clear from the NRP's report that multiple contexts and repetitions are required to "learn" a word. Word learning is like the dimmer switch on a lamp. It's not a simple matter of first not knowing a word and after instruction knowing it. Word learning occurs in degrees, as depth and breadth knowledge of the word develops. Students must experience a word many times before it becomes part of their reading vocabulary. Depending on the kind of word and the ease of visualizing its meaning, it may take up to 20 different exposures (Richek, 2003).

The research review also shows that active involvement in vocabulary learning is best. When students are engaged through multiple modalities, lessons are more effective and vocabulary is learned.

In the next sections, we will look at how to assess students' knowledge of sight words, reading vocabulary, and the word-learning strategies they use. We will also discuss ways of planning your instruction using the information you gather.

Because any formal assessment you administer will only be able to test a fraction of the words students recognize and understand, the best assessment is closely observing students as you discuss books and ideas and noticing what kinds of words they use and how well they understand the text you read. This section will give you some informal strategies for assessing knowledge of specific reading vocabulary and the strategies students use with unfamiliar words. You will also learn some formal strategies for assessing your students' sight word vocabulary and general reading vocabulary.

Sight-Word Assessment

Assessing sight word knowledge is relatively easy. There are a number of lists of common sight words available. Rebecca Sitton, Edward Fry, and Edward Dolch have all developed lists of high-frequency words. Many school districts have their own lists of words that they expect students to master in each primary grade. Whatever list you decide to use, the procedure for assessment is the same. Because students read the words aloud one at a time, it's best to do the assessment with individual students.

SIGHT WORD VOCABULARY ASSESSMENT

Procedure

1. Write the selected words on index cards. If you are using graded lists, write each grade level in a different-colored marker. Otherwise, write the lists in sets of about 20 words, in order of frequency.

2. Place the index cards on a ring, in the same order as they appear on the list.

3. Make copies of the list to record each student's answers.

4. Show each word to the student for approximately five seconds. The student should not have time to figure the word out. You want to see if he or she instantly recognizes it. If not, say the word for the student.

5. Mark a plus (+) for each word known, and a minus (−) for words missed. If you are really quick, you can write down what the student says if he or she substitutes a word, like *thought* for *though*. I'm not usually that fast.

John 9/28

Set Four	Set Five	Set Six
+ little	__ down	__ first
+ has	__ work	__ friend
+ them	__ put	__ girl
− how	__ were	__ house
+ like	__ before	__ find
+ our	__ just	__ because
− what	__ long	__ pretty
+ know	__ here	__ could
+ make	__ other	__ look
+ which	__ old	__ mother
+ much	__ take	__ people
+ who	__ again	__ school
+ an	__ give	__ night
+ their	__ after	__ say
+ she	__ saw	__ think
− new	__ home	__ where
+ said	__ soon	__ morning
+ did	__ stand	__ live
+ boy	__ box	__ four
+ three	__ upon	__ color
17 /20	__ /20	__ /20
85%		

First grader John's sight word assessment

6. If the student knows at least 80 percent of the words, go up to the next list. If he or she knows less than 50 percent of the words, go down to the next easier list.

7. Make a record of words that were difficult for each student. These will become target words for the student to work on. See pages 98–106 for activities and lessons for teaching sight words.

8. About every three or four weeks, assess the students to see if they can identify the target words, and move up to the next list for some new target words.

In the example on page 88, John was able to quickly name 17 of the 20 words from Set Four. Since he knew so many of these, he would be able to move up to the next set. The three missed words from Set Four, along with two or three missed words from Set Five, would become John's target words for instruction.

In the example below, Zoe was able to name only seven of the words from Set Two. We would ask her to try reading the words in Set One to see how many of those she knows. If she knew all of the words in this set, then five of the missed words in Set Two would become Zoe's target words for instruction.

Zoe 9/28

Set One	Set Two	Set Three
__the	⁻your	__all
__a	⁻as	__would
__is	+but	__any
__you	+be	__been
__to	+he	__out
__and	__they	__there
__we	__one	__from
__that	__good	__go
__in	+me	__see
__not	__about	__then
__for	+had	__us
__at	__if	__no
__with	__some	__him
__it	+up	__by
__on	__her	__was
__can	__do	__come
__will	__when	__get
__are	__so	__or
__of	+my	__two
__this	__very	__man
____/20	7/20 35%	____/20

First grader Zoe's sight word assessment

Reading Vocabulary Assessments

Assessing reading vocabulary is not easy. One could never even begin to teach students the thousands of words they might encounter in their reading, so it is impossible to assess how many of these words they know.

Another difficulty with assessing specific reading vocabulary is the notion of what it means to know a word. Words have many different meanings. For example, students may be familiar with the word *team*, but have no understanding of the term when it is used in the phrase *a team of horses*. They may be able to match isolated words with definitions, but not understand the meaning of sentences using the words.

There are ways to get an idea of a student's basic reading vocabulary level, however. Most Informal Reading Inventories (IRIs) have lists of words grouped according to grade level, as shown at left.

GENERAL READING VOCABULARY ASSESSMENT

Procedure

1. Select a list of words from an IRI at the student's grade level.

2. Use the same procedure for assessing sight words (pages 88–89), allowing students about five seconds to say each word aloud. Ask students to use the words they can pronounce in a sentence or give you a synonym. This will let you know if students understand at least one of the meanings of the words they recognize, and give you a truer picture of your students' word knowledge.

3. Mark a plus (+) for each word the student can pronounce. Circle the plus if he or she can also give a synonym or use the word correctly in a sentence.

4. Do not time students' responses. If students cannot pronounce the word, simply move on to the next one.

Sample Fourth Grade–Level Words

escape	pilot
desert	fame
crop	precious
islands	settlers
chief	guarded
mounds	passenger
busy	boundaries
pond	communicate
signs	adventurer
ocean	invented

From *Qualitative Reading Inventory–3*, Lauren Leslie and JoAnne Caldwell, Addison Wesley Longman, 2001.

If they can pronounce it, ask for the word's meaning and then move on to the next word.

5. Repeat the assessment with the next set of words for students with scores higher than 70 to 85 percent. Those who score below 70 percent would try the words listed for the grade level below.

This assessment gives you a rough estimate of the student's grade-level equivalent vocabulary because it is only a small sampling of possible words that most grade-level students know. Therefore, the words missed on this assessment should not become target words for the students to study in the same way as sight words.

SPECIFIC READING VOCABULARY ASSESSMENT: RESPONSE SIGNALS

For specific reading vocabulary words that you want students to know, use an informal assessment of specific words from a current or upcoming unit of study or text to plan your instruction. One of my favorite ways to do this is with student response signals, especially in guided reading groups as I introduce new vocabulary words.

Procedure

1. Write eight to ten new vocabulary words on index cards.

2. Give students three colored cubes—red, yellow, and green—and remind students that these are the colors of a traffic signal. I explain that green is the signal for go—it's smooth traveling here because you know the word. You've heard it before, you can say what it means, and you can even use it in a sentence. Yellow means slow down, be careful. Perhaps you've heard the word before, and you might even have a fuzzy idea of what it means. But you have to be careful, because things are a little shaky. Red means stop. You've never heard this word before, and you sure don't know what it means. You need to stop and use some word-learning strategies to see if you can figure it out.

3. Show students the new vocabulary words one at a time. Encourage them to apply phonics skills to figure out the pronunciation of the word.

4. Ask students to show you the red, yellow, or green cube to indicate how well they understand this word. Students who show green tell

what the word means and use it in a sentence. Students showing a yellow cube tell what they think it means. If students think they know the meaning of a word and they really don't, you will, of course, clear up any misconceptions.

5. If the student holds up red, you will need to do a thorough job of introducing the vocabulary word, offering many different examples and contexts. See pages 106–113 for ways to introduce new vocabulary words.

Whole-Class Written Variation

If you prefer, you can do the assessment of new reading vocabulary in a written form. This is especially effective for vocabulary words your whole class will be learning for a particular subject. You can give this assessment to your whole class at once. Provide a worksheet with the words, circles, and a line for sentences. Students will also need crayons in red, yellow, and green. Ask students to color the circle next to each word to show their level of understanding, and to provide a sentence for words they know, as shown in the example from Nathan below.

○ matter _It doesn't matter._

● mass _____

○ atom _____

● element _____

● particles _____

○ conduct_____

◐ insulate _My coat insulates me._

◐ compound_Two words put together is a compound._

● density _____

Fifth grader Nathan "signals" that he knows several science terms.

Nathan has some experience with two of the given science terms that will help him with the upcoming unit: He knows meanings for *insulate* and *compound*. The meaning he gives for *matter* is inaccurate in this context. Although students have had experience with physical science units in prior grades, it is obvious that this boy will have to learn much of the new vocabulary he'll encounter in this unit.

This informal assessment is a good way to create some need-based groups for vocabulary instruction. You can work intensively with groups of students who are unfamiliar with most of the upcoming vocabulary, and have the more capable students create some vocabulary cards to help teach the other students. This is described in Picture This/Vocabulary Cards (page 109).

Word-Learning Strategies Assessments

Word-learning strategies are vital to a student's comprehension of the many words he or she will encounter in texts. I find it useful to assess the strategies students use when figuring out unknown words. An individual interview seems to work the best for me. I try to do this during a reading conference or independent reading time. You can also informally assess younger students as you talk together about word-solving strategies in a guided reading lesson.

INFORMAL WORD-LEARNING STRATEGIES ASSESSMENT

This is an assessment that can be done during independent reading with individual students.

Procedure

1. Select an unfamiliar text at your student's appropriate reading level.

2. Preview the text to make sure it contains some unfamiliar words.

3. Ask the student to read the text, paying special attention to words that he or she found challenging. Ask the student to be ready to discuss how he or she figured out those words. The student can also jot down the words and the strategy used in his or her writing journal.

4. Then have the student share with you the words he or she identified as challenging, and the strategies used to figure them out. Keep notes of what strategies the student used effectively. You are looking for a combination

of solutions that draw on the context of the text, the support of pictures, and word analysis, as shown in the Tools Used section of the recording form below (reproducible form on page 95).

5. Select a few words to discuss with students who finish the selected text and tell you that all of the words were easy and they didn't have to work any of them out. I ask these students to pronounce the words I've selected, and tell me what they think they mean. It often turns out they weren't so sure about some of these words. As one of my students sometimes says to me, "I knew it when I read, but I just forgot when you asked me." Students who consistently respond this way are often simply skipping the words. You will need to keep an eye on their comprehension skills, as discussed in Chapter 5, and provide instruction on how to search for meaning as they read.

Student Tim			Text Aladdin			Date 12/7		
Word	Selected by		Meaning			Tools Used		
	Student	Teacher	Full	Partial	Low	Context	Picture	Word analysis
underground	Ⓢ	T	X					X
cavern	Ⓢ	T	X			X	X	
collapsed	Ⓢ	T	X			X		
scornfully	S	Ⓣ		X				X
immediately	S	Ⓣ		X		X		X
	S	T						
	S	T						
	S	T						

Unfamiliar words from the short story "Aladdin" and the strategies fourth grader Tim used to figure out their meanings.

The more your student can tell you about how he or she figured out the words, the more data you'll have to plan instruction. As Tim and I discussed the words from "Aladdin," I learned that Tim found the two parts of the compound word *underground* and used them to determine the meaning (a word-analysis strategy). He was also able to use the context of the sentence along with the accompanying picture to determine that *cavern* meant *cave*. He used sentence context again to determine the meaning of *collapsed*. While he applied word analysis again, using word parts to decode the words *immediately* and *scornfully*, he was not able to use *-ful* or *-ly* to completely understand the meaning of these adverbs. Although he used the context of the sentence to determine that *immediately* meant *right away*, he wasn't sure why the word had an *-ly* ending. He

WORD-LEARNING STRATEGIES RECORD

Student _____ Text _____ Date _____

Word	Selected by Student Teacher	Meaning Full Partial Low	Tools Used Context Picture Word analysis
	S T		
	S T		
	S T		
	S T		
	S T		
	S T		
	S T		
	S T		
	S T		

✂ ···

Student _____ Text _____ Date _____

Word	Selected by Student Teacher	Meaning Full Partial Low	Tools Used Context Picture Word analysis
	S T		
	S T		
	S T		
	S T		
	S T		
	S T		
	S T		
	S T		
	S T		

knew that *scornfully* meant *rude*, but also was confused about the use of *-ful* with the base word *scorn*.

This word-learning strategies assessment will give you a general idea of what students do when they encounter new reading vocabulary. It does not guarantee that they effectively use the strategies in every situation. After analyzing the results, you may discover some students only use context clues effectively, and don't use word parts to determine meanings. Your data will help you to create need-based groups or design whole-class instruction. For example, I would place Tim, from the sample above, in a group to work with the suffixes *-ful* and *-ly*, and also in a group for guided practice using context clues when there are no pictures to help. See the chart on page 97 for some specific activities.

PLAN

Once you've got some assessment data, it's time to plan your instruction. In some cases, you will teach, clarify, or provide practice with high-frequency words and reading vocabulary to large or small groups of students. You may need to teach word-learning strategies to your whole class. Your data will show which strategies your students most often rely on, and which areas you need to develop. You may find some children who will need individualized, intensive instruction.

Based on your assessments of sight words, notice patterns that show which words are difficult for your students. Identify target words that students have not yet mastered. You may be able to select some common words to work on for the whole class or small groups, perhaps through a word wall or direct instruction with magnetic letters or games. In addition to group sight-word activities, I often have students practice their individualized target words several times a week during centers or independent work time, either with Sight Word Phrases (page 104) or Word Shapes (page 105).

Next, look at the general level of vocabulary knowledge in your class as indicated by the grade-level reading vocabulary tests. Do some students have a grade-level vocabulary far lower than others in your class? Remember, this is just an indicator. You may decide that general vocabulary development is a priority for your whole class or for targeted small groups.

Look at the word-learning strategies students are currently using with difficult words. Do students need instruction in particular strategies? Would your whole class benefit from further instruction and practice with word analysis? You may plan modeling lessons or cloze activities with small or large groups of students several times a week. Again, you may find individual students who need intense instruction in this area, with very guided practice and much coaching during reading conferences.

If the child . . .	Then you might try . . .	Page number
has difficulty reading common sight words	Sight Word Wall	98
	Guess My Word	100
	Word Chain	101
	Rainbow Wordo	101
	Sight Word Phrases	104
	Magnetic Letters	104
	Word Shapes	105
	Reading Easy or Familiar Books	106
has a limited reading vocabulary	Introducing . . . Key Vocabulary!	107
	Picture This/Vocabulary Cards	109
	Word Webs	110
	Read Related Texts	111
	Teacher Read-Aloud and Harvesting of Words	111
	Wide Reading or Books on Tape	112
does not use word-learning strategies to figure out unknown words	Modeling the Use of Word Parts	113
	Make-a-Word Game	116
	Modeling the Use of Context Clues	118
	Guess the Covered Word	118
	Cloze Passages	119
	Interesting Words Chart	120

Finally, use your informal assessments of reading vocabulary to tailor your introduction and teaching of specific reading vocabulary. Remember that research suggests practicing words many times in multiple contexts.

The chart on page 97 will help you plan instructional activities for students who are having difficulties with specific areas of vocabulary learning. Each activity is described in the following section.

Sight Word Activities

The following collection of activities will help students develop sight word vocabulary. Select the words for the activities based on the results of your assessments. You can also group students with similar needs for more individualized word practice.

SIGHT WORD WALL (Large or small group, individual)

A classroom wall is a perfect place to prominently display a collection of high-frequency sight words. Students use the wall as a reference for reading and writing. The words come from the list of words that you've used to assess students (pages 87–89), and they should be printed on paper or sentence strips and appear large enough to be seen by students sitting at their desks. You can also make smaller word walls for individuals or small groups by printing the words inside a file folder. Your students can keep these in their desks or you can use them during guided reading or writing groups. You can personalize these smaller word walls by including the target words each student needs to learn.

● Let your word wall grow throughout the year. Begin the year with a wall that is blank except for the alphabet letters, spaced so that words can be grouped beneath them. Introduce about six words each week and place them up on the wall underneath their starting letter, as in the example on page 99.

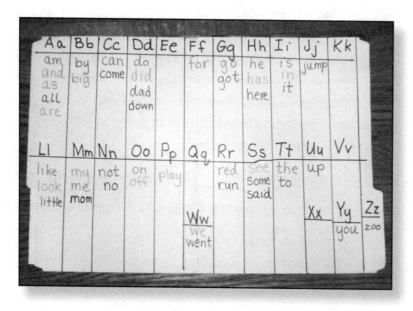

An individualized word wall can be created with a file folder and kept at a student's desk.

- Choose words for your wall that cause difficulty for many students, but also put up some words that they all know, too. This will help all students feel successful right away as you use the words for the activities explained on pages 100–106.

- Make the words as visually accessible as possible. Many teachers write the words on different-colored paper and cut around the shape of the words. The different colors make it easier for students to locate words on the wall. For example, you can help a student looking for the word *went* by narrowing the choices a little and saying, "It's one of the green words under *W*."

- Make introducing new words for the word wall part of your weekly routine.

Steps for Introducing Word Wall Words

1. Show the word you've written on paper.

2. Tell students the word.

3. Use the word in a sentence. For younger students, I also like to locate the word on a chart or in a big book, so they can see it in print surrounded by other words. You can also ask students to use the word in their own sentence.

4. Say the letters. For younger students or those who are really strug-gling to remember, I like to act out the letters, like this: Hands up in

the air for tall letters, hands on my hips for one-space letters, and lean over and touch the floor (or your knees) for letters that go below the line and have tails. So the word "they" would be spelled "t"—hands up, "h" —hands up, "e" —hands on hips, and "y" —bend over. We call this spelling cheerleading. For those students who struggle to learn words, involving their whole bodies in this way provides a way to "hook" the words into their brains.

5. Have students form imaginary letters in the air as they spell the words aloud.

6. Have students write the word on a whiteboard or piece of paper as they say the letters.

7. Place the word card on the word wall under the correct starting letter.

8. Repeat steps with next word.

9. Once words are posted on the word wall, provide daily opportunities for students to use them. You will find dozens of ideas in professional books specifically about word wall activities, including those listed at left. Here are three of my favorite ideas for practicing the words.

GUESS MY WORD (Large or small group, individual)

You can fit this activity in whenever you have a few extra minutes.

● Select a word on the word wall and provide hints to students. You can use any kind of clues you want, depending on what you want students to focus on. Here's an example:

   ○ I'm thinking of a word on the word wall that starts with *t*.

   ○ It also ends with *t*.

   ○ It has one letter that goes below the line.

   ○ It has two silent consonants.

   ○ It goes in this sentence: "I _____ I had my library book, but I forgot it at home."

   That's right, the word is *thought*.

● As you give clues, ask students to write their guesses down and share them with the whole group or partners. Notice that the last clue makes everyone successful at figuring out the word.

WORD CHAIN (Large or small group, individual)

This activity works well as a center or as an individual or group project once you've done it together a few times.

● Begin by selecting any word from the word wall.

● Ask students to find and write another word from the wall "that begins the way the first word ends" (begins with the final letter of the first word). For example, if you chose *this* to start with, the next word might be *should*.

● Continue locating and writing words from the word wall in the same way, until students run out of words that fit the pattern.

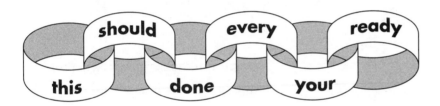

In a word chain, students link sight words by matching
the last letter of one word to the first letter of another.

Students enjoy seeing how long they can make the chain, and are motivated to try many different words in order to make a longer chain than other groups of students. Because students are searching the word wall over and over to see what's there, they get a chance to read many of the word wall words over and over again.

RAINBOW WORDO (Large or small group)

This game is played like bingo, using word wall words. Students will need a pencil, and several colors of markers or crayons for tracing.

● To prepare the boards, distribute copies of page 103 to students and have them use a pencil to fill in the grid with words chosen from the word wall. To ensure that students all have the same words on their grids in different arrangements, fill the board in together. Take turns with the students choosing words from the word wall. Have students write their words on the board in any square they like, chanting the letters as they write out each word. Write the words the class selects on cards that you can use to call out the words.

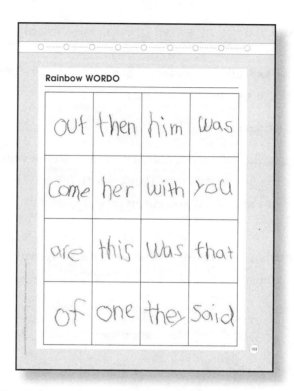

A WORDO board ready for the first round.

- For the first round, decide on a light-color marker or crayon, such as yellow, for students to use to trace the words as they find them.

- Give clues for each word. For example, you might say, "The first word has two syllables and it means 'in front of.' That's right, it's the word *before*. Find it and write over the letters." Students then trace over the letters of the word with a yellow marker or crayon. "The next word fits in this sentence: I ____ my lunch to school today. That's right, it's *brought*." Your clues can be cloze-type sentences, rhyming words, parts of speech, or anything you want to focus on.

- Continue in this way until someone has a wordo (bingo). That student reads his or her outlined words and then gets a yellow star for being the winner.

- Select a different-color marker, perhaps red this time, for students to use for tracing the selected words. The first player to get a wordo with all red outlined words is the winner and gets a red star.

- Continue in the same way with other colors. When you've finished the game, the words are outlined as if they were a rainbow.

This game provides excellent practice with spelling and identifying unique features of the words, and you can tailor the clues to target any skills your students need to practice.

Rainbow WORDO

SIGH WORD PHRASES (Large or small group, individual)

Because many sight words do not have much meaning on their own, students easily confuse them, for example, substituting *for* in place of the word *of*. It helps students to practice the words in common phrases that they might see in text. For example, *of* and *for* are often confused. Reading the phrases *some for me* and *a kind of* helps students to fix the usage of each word in their minds. See the list at left for some phrases to use with some of the first 100 sight words, appropriate for first graders and struggling readers at other grades. Make similar phrases for target words your students are studying.

Write these phrases on cards, and use them as flash cards or in games, just as you might use word cards. Each student can have his or her own ring of these phrases, featuring target words to practice reading whenever they can—during work time, centers, or independent reading time. Reading the phrases to a partner is a great warm-up for a guided reading group. Add new phrases as the student's target words change. You can take off the cards students have mastered, or move them to another ring as evidence of the growing number of words they know.

MAGNETIC LETTERS (Small group, individual)

When beginning readers are having difficulty learning specific sight words, using magnetic letters can be very helpful. Students can quickly learn to spell and recognize the words as they manipulate the letters. Because I only give students the letters necessary for making the target word, they can focus on the order of the letters within a word, rather than trying to remember what the letters are. Here's an effective way to use the letters.

- Choose a word to focus on and write the word on a card.

- Show children the card and say the word.

- Ask children to name the letters in the word in order, and repeat the word while looking at the card.

- Give each child the magnetic letters that spell the word. I often have them ready in a small cup.

- Hide the card and ask children to make the word with the letters, and run their finger under the word while they read it.

- Ask, "Were you right?" Let them check with the card.

- Ask children to mix the letters up, rebuild the word without looking at the card, and check it again.

- Repeat this process with the word until the children are successful several times in a row. As they practice, ask them to look hard and remember what comes first in the word, what is in the middle, and what is last.

- Cover up the letters and ask children to write the word.

- Finally, show children some written text, and ask them to locate the word in the text. Remind children this is a word they will see many times, and will want to be able to read quickly.

- When reading new text containing the word, ask children to look quickly to find the word before they begin to read the whole text.

This particular activity also works well as a center, if you place one word on the cover of a small box or envelope, and the magnetic letters for the word inside. Students can use the letters to build the word and check the example on the outside. Put the words your students need the most help with in the center.

WORD SHAPES (Large or small group, individual)

For some children, seeing the shape of the word is very helpful. Just as we focused on tall letters, one-space letters, and below-the-line letters when we introduced words for the word wall, and we cut around the outline of each word to highlight its shape on the word wall, students can focus on word shapes by writing letters into shape boxes when practicing the words. Sometimes having shape boxes helps students move from magnetic letters to being able to recognize the word more easily in print. For each word you are practicing, draw boxes that match the letter shapes, like this:

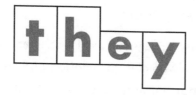

This is another activity that works well as a center, particularly if you have target words written on cards, and shapes made from tagboard. Students can build the words by placing magnetic letters on the appropriate shape.

Sight Word Resources

Perfect Poems for Teaching Sight Words by D. Ellermeyer & J. Rowell

Poems for Sight Word Practice by L. Reynolds

Sight Word Poetry by Teacher Created Resources

Sight Word Poetry Pages by R. Williams

READING EASY OR FAMILIAR BOOKS
(Large or small group, individual)

Because sight words are words that occur over and over in text, rereading familiar or easy text is an excellent way for students to develop their sight word vocabulary. Encourage students to spend part of each day reading text that is very easy for them, but not so easy that they don't have to look at the text. We don't want students to say, as one of mine did, "Look, I can read this book with my eyes closed!"

I usually begin my guided reading group lessons with time for independent or shared rereading of familiar books or poems. Beginning readers read simple short books and poems, while students in grades 3 through 5 read favorite poems. This is both a good review of sight words and an effective means to develop fluency that gives students an immediate feeling of success. It is also an excellent time for students to check these texts for the presence and frequency of their target words. See the list of books at left for some good teaching resources for poetry and sight word development.

Specific Reading Vocabulary Activities

What about improving reading vocabulary? Which of the words should be taught before reading, and how do we go about it? Let's see how to make those decisions.

Which Words?

It is tempting to teach lots of new vocabulary words in preparation for new text. However, introducing more than 10 words or so is not effective; this is too much new information for students to remember. You need to make some careful decisions about which words to introduce before reading a particular text. Here are three things I keep in mind when deciding which ones to select.

- **The word must be necessary for understanding the selection.** For example, if a text is about a family coming to America and the trouble they face, it would be important that students be familiar with the vocabulary word *immigrant*.

- **The word must be useful.** That is, this word is likely to appear in other texts students read. Consider these words selected for preteaching in a teachers' edition of an anthology of fourth-grade literature: *tuft* and *nocturnal*. The word *tuft* isn't critical to students' understanding of the story (*tuft of grass*) and they aren't likely to see it again soon. We simply clarified that word later as we read. *Nocturnal*, however, occurs in many other contexts and is therefore highly useful. This is the word to introduce before reading.

● **The word cannot be determined through context or word analysis.** For example, a group of third-grade students recently read a text about pirates that included two new words: *mangled* and *mast*. In the story, a hurricane mangled the mast of the ship. There was a wonderful picture accompanying this section, and students were able to figure out what both of these words meant by using the picture and surrounding text. I did not have to preteach the words. On the other hand, the meaning of the word *buccaneer* is not clear from context or word analysis, so it needed direct instruction.

INTRODUCING . . . KEY VOCABULARY!
(Large or small group, individual)

The way you initially teach words will look different depending on the level of your readers. Because emergent readers are used to picture books, it works very well to use those pictures as you introduce the words. For more capable readers, you may need to bring in pictures when appropriate and make sure to provide very thorough explanations of other selected vocabulary words. There are several things to remember for your initial instruction of reading vocabulary:

● Introduce the words with more than one example and a definition

● Show how the new words connect with known words and concepts

● Actively involve students

Let's see what this might look like with students of different reading abilities.

Introduction and Definition

For emergent readers, begin with a picture walk through the text. As you lead students through the book, highlight vocabulary words and link the words to the pictures, like this:

> "The boy was feeling very *cross*. That word *cross* is
> an interesting word. Here it is right here. Look at the

picture. See his face? How do you think he's feeling? That's right, he looks very mad. *Cross* is another word that means *mad*."

For more fluent readers, you might display a sentence using the key word. Help students to decode the word using word parts and chunks. Explain the meaning like this:

"The sentence says, 'The shark is a dangerous *predator*.' A *predator* is an animal that attacks and kills other animals for food. We call the animals that it kills its *prey*. Sharks kill and eat fish and seals, so the shark is a *predator* and its *prey* is fish and seals."

Multiple Contexts

Next, provide other contexts for the word by giving some examples of your own. For younger students, you might say,

"I sometimes feel cross when my cat scratches on the door in the night. It wakes me up and I get a little mad at him. Sometimes I get cross when my newspaper is delivered late so I can't read it before I come to school. I feel kind of grumpy. When do you feel cross? Finish this sentence, 'I feel *cross* when_____.'"

For older students, you might say,

"There are many kinds of predators. Some are big and some are small. Spiders are predators. They kill and eat insects, so their prey is insects. They catch them in their webs. Do you know other animals that are predators? See if you can finish this sentence, ' A _____ is a *predator* and its prey is _____.'"

Is It or Isn't It?

After using the word in other situations, ask students to decide if the vocabulary word fits different situations.

"Would you feel cross if you got a new toy? Would you feel cross if you broke your favorite toy? Your mother just mopped the kitchen floor and you came in with muddy feet. Will she feel cross?"

For older students:

> "A cow eats grass. Is it a predator? You give your dog his food in a bowl. Is he a predator? Your cat catches mice. Is she a predator? Sometimes we talk about people being predators. This kind of predator doesn't attack and kill animals, but they use people in other ways that are bad. For example, long ago pirates attacked and robbed other ships. People called them predators. Do you think that someone who sold drugs to young people might be called a predator?"

Show It

To actively involve the students, I invite them to perform some actions related to the vocabulary words. For example, "Show how your face and body might look if you were cross" or "Show how a predator might look running after its prey."

Once you have introduced several words, ask students to act out a word, and invite other students to guess which word is being represented. This is a wonderful way to get students involved in thinking about the words. When vocabulary words are not verbs or nouns they are not easily conveyed. It is fascinating to see the variety of ways students show word meanings.

PICTURE THIS/VOCABULARY CARDS
(Large or small group, individual)

After several vocabulary words have been introduced, or as a review, I like to have students sketch and label pictures in their writing journals to represent the words. This way they have a resource to refer to later if they forget what a word means. Ask students to write the word in their journals, and draw a picture to represent the word, along with a sentence explaining the picture.

Students can also make vocabulary cards, with the word and picture on the outside of a folded piece of paper. Inside, students write a definition and sentence to go with the vocabulary word. For example, a card for *reservoir* might have the word and a picture of a large lake. Inside would be the sentence, *We drove by a large reservoir of water in the mountains,* and the definition: *a place for storing water.*

WORD WEBS (Large or small group, individual)

A word web is an effective tool for developing in-depth word knowledge and forging connections between vocabulary words and existing knowledge. To create a word web, select a target vocabulary word, and add lines radiating out from the word like spokes of a wheel. Students suggest related words, and the teacher helps to organize words into categories. Students add additional words to the different categories, using synonyms or other related words, as shown in the web for the vocabulary word *predator* below. Students contributed many ideas, including words for specific predators, things they do, and body parts that help them attack other animals.

Although this sample web was created by a group of fourth graders and uses sophisticated content area language, word webs are a valuable vocabulary activity for primary students, too. Once students understand how to create a web, they can work independently or in small groups. It is also an excellent tool for assessing students' knowledge about content area vocabulary and concepts both before and after a unit. Some teachers provide lists of vocabulary and ask students to use the words as part of the web they are creating.

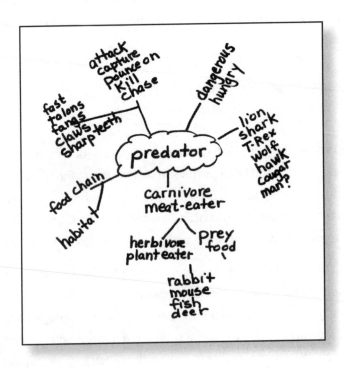

Word web for *predator*

READ RELATED TEXTS (Large or small group, individual)

Because words have to be heard, seen, and read multiple times to be remembered and known, reading related texts is an excellent way to give students more practice with vocabulary words and concepts. The related texts offer repetition of some vocabulary words in similar contexts, plus other related words. Researcher Camille Blachowicz, as mentioned earlier in this chapter (see page 85), suggests using a series of five related texts. Gathering a collection of words around a topic and listening for those words in additional texts has been found to be helpful for children's vocabulary development. As each book is read, additional words can be added to existing lists or word webs. Here are two ways to structure work with related texts.

● Pair a nonfiction text with a fiction selection. For example, when reading an old favorite like *Charlotte's Web* (E. B. White, 1952), you might also read *Be Nice to Spiders* (Margaret Bloy Graham, 1967) or an informational article about spiders. If your selections are about spiders, there will be repetition of words like *web*, *spin*, *silk*, and *spinnerets*. The nonfiction selection will provide students with background knowledge and vocabulary that will assist them in reading and comprehending the fiction text. Any of these companion texts can be used as a teacher read-aloud, a shared reading, or in a guided reading group

● Gather a selection of related texts for students to read during independent reading time. If you choose this option, it is very important to give students time to share what they learned or a connection they made while reading. That way, other students will benefit from what their classmates have learned, plus it will give the original reader another chance to use the vocabulary.

General Vocabulary Development Activities

By second grade, the difference between the number of known words among students can be as many as 4,000 words (Biemiller, 2004). The gap widens as students get older. However, there are ways to increase your students' general word knowledge. The following activities have been effective for me.

TEACHER READ-ALOUD AND HARVESTING OF WORDS (Large group)

Many words are learned from reading books and seeing words in multiple contexts. Even struggling students learn new vocabulary words this way. In this activity, you do the reading. Keep in mind that for children in the primary grades especially, reading the same text more than once contributes more to vocabulary development than reading different texts (Coyne, Simmons, & Kame'enui, 2004).

- Set time aside each day to read aloud several texts, both fiction and nonfiction, and discuss the interesting ideas, concepts, and vocabulary words that the text includes. Revisit old favorites, along with new books.

- Select three to five key vocabulary words to discuss during and after you read the book. (Remember, it is most effective to select Tier 2 words, words that are relatively sophisticated but appear in many different contexts.) Locate the words in the book, and provide definitions.

- Make a chart of these "harvested" words. Keep tally marks on the chart to show how often the class hears or reads these words in the course of a week. It's amazing the way children hear words in the context of a story and suddenly begin hearing and using the same words in many different situations.

For example, I recently read a group of second-grade students *Me First*, by Helen Lester (1992). After reading, we found the following interesting words: *faint, distance, notice, privilege, concerning*. After discussing the words and placing them on a chart, we kept an eye (and ear) out for the words. At the end of the week we had found them all several times in other books or conversations. In fact, students began using the words appropriately in their own conversations, and even in their writing.

While every read-aloud text doesn't need to be followed by a formal vocabulary lesson, harvesting a few interesting words each day can add significantly to your students' general vocabulary. Learning just three words a day can increase a student's vocabulary level by more than 400 words in the course of a school year.

WIDE READING OR BOOKS ON TAPE
(Small group or individual)

Because reading vocabulary is developed through lots of exposure to words, the single most important thing students can do is read a lot. However, many students do not read outside of class, or if they do, they skip over difficult or unfamiliar words. Making time for independent reading is time well spent.

- Set aside 15 to 20 minutes each day for students to read independently and talk about what they read with others.

- Ask students to locate interesting words to share with their partners or small groups. For students in grades 3 through 5 it is highly motivating to try to stump their groups by locating words unfamiliar to everyone else. For those students with limited reading skills, listening to books on tape and following along in a text can also help develop vocabulary. Give students key words to listen for in the text and ask them to determine the meanings of the words using word-learning strategies, as discussed below.

Activities for Developing Word-Learning Strategies

There are three basic vocabulary strategies students will need to learn for new words: structural analysis, context, and dictionary use.

Structural Analysis Strategies

Structural analysis is using the root word and word parts to determine the meaning of an unfamiliar word. To students in second grade and higher, learning common roots, prefixes, and suffixes is a great help as they encounter new words in their reading. There are many affixes and roots, so teaching the most common ones will help students the most. The chart on page 114 shows some of the most common affixes and their meanings.

You will notice that several affixes have the same meaning. For younger students, begin with the most common, such as *un-* for *not*, and *-er* for *one who*. Teaching these affixes will require direct instruction and modeling, linking this new knowledge to students' existing knowledge, and giving multiple examples.

As you begin, use root words that are familiar to students. Students in grades 4 and higher can learn common Greek and Latin roots, some of which are listed in the chart on page 115. Following are some activities that help students apply what they are learning about word parts.

MODELING THE USE OF WORD PARTS
(Large or small group, individual)

Many students have no idea how to use structural analysis during reading, so it is important that you model this for them within the context of reading. Keep in mind that before you can expect students to use this strategy on their

Common Prefixes and Suffixes

Affix	Meaning	Example
un-, dis-, in-, il-, mis-, non-	not, the opposite of	dislike, unhappy, invisible, illegal, misplace
re-	again	redo
over-	too much	overdone
under-	below, too little	undercover
-less	without	helpless
-ful	full of	helpful
-tion, -ion, -ation, -ition	act of doing	action, construction, operation, demolition
-ly	like, in that way	friendly
-able, -ible	capable or worth	lovable, collectible
-al, -ial	of, relating to	parental, partial
-y	consisting of	furry
-ness	condition	brightness
-er, -or	one who	teacher, sailor

Adapted from *The Struggling Reader*, Cooper, Chard, and Kiger, 2006.

own while reading, you will have to model this sequence over and over again, inviting students to help you locate the different parts and their meanings.

- As you are reading aloud to students or during shared reading, stop occasionally to work out an unfamiliar word. You might say something like this, "I'm not quite sure of that word right there. I think I might have heard of it before, but I better take a harder look at it."

- You might stop here and write the word on a whiteboard for students to see, and explain how to break the word into meaningful parts. For example, "Here is the word—*disagreeable*. It's awfully long. I can see some parts at the beginning and the end that have been added to a little word in the middle. I can see *dis-* which I know means *not*, the same as in *dislike*, and

I see -*able*, like in *readable*, which means 'someone should be able to read it.' The root word is *agree*, and I know what that means. So it looks like this word means 'not able to agree.' Let's see if that makes sense in the sentence, 'The old man was rude and disagreeable.' I think I'm right, because if you are rude, you might also be hard to agree with. I've got it."

● With beginning readers in grades 1 and 2, model structural analysis using compound words and words with endings such as -*ing*, -*ed*, and -*s*. Toward the end of grade 2, use structural analysis with prefixes and suffixes. Often your state standards will specify which prefixes and suffixes should be taught at each grade level. You can also find guidelines in district-level curriculum and/or the teacher's editions for grade-level reading anthologies.

Common Roots and Their Meanings

Root	Meaning	Example
port	to carry	portable (able to be moved)
struct	build	structure (something that was built)
prim	first	primary (first, most important)
dict	to say	contradict (say something against)
ject	throw	reject (throw out)
voc	voice, to call	vocal (using a voice)
astro	star	astronomer (one who studies the stars)
auto	self	autobiography (a story of oneself)
phono	sound	telephone (a device to carry sound)
graph	write	autograph (a written signature)

MAKE-A-WORD GAME (Small group or individual)

This activity asks students to construct words with affixes. The practice of building words will help students use affixes to determine word meanings during reading. You will need cards made from three colors of paper for the word parts, and pencils and paper to record the words students make. You can select your own affixes and root words or use the ones provided on page 117.

● Write an assortment of prefixes on cards made from one color. On a set of cards made with another color, put endings.

● On cards of a third color, write some root words.

● Ask students to choose a root word and try to build as many words as they can by adding prefixes and endings to that word. Students record each word on paper, and either define the word or write a sentence using the word.

You can also change this activity into a group game by following these directions:

● The first person selects a root word.

● The next person adds to the word with a prefix or ending that makes a real word, and tells what the word means.

● The next person changes a card or adds a tile to make a new word and says what it means.

● Building new words, students continue as long as they can.

● Each time a card is used, it is placed in a "used card pile."

● When students have made as many words as they can, count all the cards in the used card pile. This is their score.

● Begin again with a new root word. Try to get a higher score this time.

Context Strategies

Context refers to using the surrounding sentences in a text to determine the meaning of an unfamiliar word. Here are several activities that will help students to develop this strategy.

Make-a-Word Activity

Prefixes	Root Words		Endings	
re-	agree	help	-s	-ment
dis-	clean	light	-es	-less
un-	clear	member	-d	-ful
over-	count	miss	-ed	-y
mis-	cover	part	-ing	-able
under-	dress	play	-er	-ness
	fresh	short	-est	
	friend	slow	-ly	
	hard	turn		

MODELING THE USE OF CONTEXT CLUES
(Large or small group)

Students at all grade levels will benefit from your modeling of context use, just as when you model structural analysis.

● During shared reading or read-aloud time, stop occasionally to work out the meaning of words that you think are unfamiliar to your students. For example, you might say, "This story said that the dog *lunged* at the squirrel. I'm not sure of the word *lunged*. I'm going to stop and think about the rest of the sentence and what is happening to see if I can figure out the word. I do know that it's something the dog did. And I know that dogs like to chase squirrels. That dog is on a leash, though, so he can't actually chase it. I think he's probably jumping toward the squirrel. I'm thinking about my dogs, and they do that when we are walking together. *Lunge* could also mean *bark*, but I've heard of people doing an exercise called a lunge where they go forward on their legs, so I think it must mean to jump forward."

● Your students will need many examples as you think aloud. After modeling several times, invite students to share their thinking aloud. After much practice, they will be able to use context independently.

GUESS THE COVERED WORD (Large or small group)

This activity leads your students to use context and sentence structure to figure out unknown words, which are exactly the skills you want them to have when reading independently.

● Select a word the students will be able to figure out using context clues and, on the board or chart paper, write a sentence using that word in context.

● Cover the word in two sections, so you can display the beginning part of the word and then the rest of the word, like this:

> Our class got very ◻ when we went on the field trip.

● Ask students to read the sentence, and skip over the covered word.

● Have students guess the covered word, and list the words to the side of the sentence. As each word is suggested, ask why it makes sense.

Accept all answers that make sense. For example, you might have the following words listed for the sample sentence:

loud	informed	wet
naughty	busy	cold
bored	exhausted	hungry
excited	tired	lost

- Then uncover the beginning letter or letters of the word (depending on how much information you want the students to have) and have students tell you which words from the list to eliminate. Cross these out.

Our class got very ex ⬚ when we went on the field trip.

- Ask for new ideas that fit the beginning *ex-*.

- Uncover the rest of the word to let students check their answer:

Our class got very excited when we went on the field trip.

Guess the Covered Word requires students who usually use only phonics with unknown words to use the context of the sentence first and their phonics skills second. It requires the same process as using context for determining the meaning of unfamiliar words when reading independently.

CLOZE PASSAGES (Large or small group, individual)

For students who are still struggling with using context clues, a cloze passage can be very useful.

- Select a paragraph at the students' independent reading level and delete selected words from the passage, leaving blank spaces.

- Ask students to read through the passage and fill in words that make sense in the blanks.

- Check that the substituted words make sense. Students do not have to put in the original words; they simply must make sense in the context of the passage.

This is also an effective comprehension activity, particularly with a text the students have previously read. It functions somewhat like a retelling, as shown in the example on the next page.

One day Goldilocks went for a walk in the _____.
She came to a little _____. She _____ on the door.
There was no answer, but she pushed open the _____
and went inside anyway.

First she saw three _____ of _____ on the table.
She _____ the first one, but it was too hot. _____
she tried the second one. It was _____ cold. Finally
she tasted the _____ one. It was just right, so she
_____ it all up.

As students compare and justify their responses with partners or groups, it will stimulate more oral language. When students discuss their answers, they may learn synonyms for their responses. For example, the first blank in the example above may be filled in by *forest* or *woods*, while the second blank may be filled in with *hut*, *house*, *cottage*, or *cabin*. When students explain their choices and discuss their differences, other students have opportunities to deepen their understanding of the selected words, as well.

Dictionary Use Strategies

Finally, students need to know how to use a dictionary. The difficulty is that there are often multiple meanings for words, and the definitions are often even more difficult to understand than the original word in context. It is hard for students to decide which meaning might fit with a particular sentence. Just as you need to spend a lot of time modeling and supporting the use of structural analysis and context, helping your students effectively use the dictionary will take time. The activity below provides modeling and guided practice for selecting appropriate dictionary definitions.

INTERESTING WORDS CHART
(Large or small group, individual)

Beginning in second grade, with your guided reading groups or during teacher read-aloud time, follow this procedure to help students make the best use of the dictionary to help them learn words.

● Select an unfamiliar word or a familiar word used in an unfamiliar way.

● Use context and structural analysis (see the modeling activities above) to develop an idea of what the word means.

- Then turn to the dictionary to see which given meaning of the word fits the context of the sentence. For example, a group of fourth graders I worked with were reading text about the early Negro League of baseball. The word *league* was unfamiliar to my students, and important for the story. Given the context, they thought it might mean a group of teams. When we looked up the word in the dictionary, we found three meanings. We chose "a class of competition" as the meaning for the word as it was used in our story. We followed the same procedure for the word *allowed*, creating the chart shown below.

- As students become more proficient at this activity, give them a form with some words and page numbers filled in and have them determine meanings for these selected words. Leave room for students to also add words they choose.

Our Interesting Words Chart

Page	Word	Meaning clues	What we think it means	What the dictionary says (meaning that fits)
3	league	The Negroes formed a *league* of their own.	a group of teams that play each other	a class of competition
4	allowed	The team members were not *allowed* to eat at the same restaurant as the manager.	let	to permit

Struggling Readers

Struggling readers often have problems with vocabulary. Your assessments will be crucial. You may find that they know few high-frequency words, have a low general vocabulary, and have few strategies for determining meanings of unfamiliar words. You might consider forming small intervention groups for vocabulary strategy instruction and guided practice after your modeling sessions. Remember that students must have experience with new vocabulary multiple times and in multiple contexts to learn the words. Extra practice sessions will be very important for students who have little experience with target reading vocabulary. Using strategies such as acting out and drawing images related to vocabulary words is very effective for struggling readers. It is time well spent, especially if you select words that are of high utility and will be seen many times in students' independent reading.

Final Thoughts

Vocabulary knowledge is crucial in the other areas of reading, and it is an area that requires time for assessing and providing targeted instruction. Once we know what types of words and word-learning strategies students are having difficulty with, we can design active lessons that provide students many opportunities to read and experience words in a variety of contexts.

Having a larger vocabulary will help students maintain meaning and fluency as they read. In the next chapter, we will focus on other ways to develop fluency, and some methods to check on how your students are doing.

Resources and Further Reading

Baumann, J. F., Kame'enui, E. J., & Ash, G. E. (2003). Research on vocabulary instruction: Voltaire redux. In J. Flood, D. Lapp, J. R. Squire, & J. M. Jensen (Eds.), *Handbook of research on teaching the English language arts* (2nd ed.). Mahwah, NJ: Erlbaum.

Beck, I., McKeown, M., & Kucan, L. (2002). *Bringing words to life.* New York: Guilford Press.

Biemiller, A. (2004). Teaching vocabulary in the primary grades: Vocabulary instruction needed. In J. F. Baumann & E. J. Kame'enui (Eds.), *Vocabulary instruction: Research to practice* (pp. 28–40). New York: Guilford Press.

Blachowicz, C. & Orbrochta, C. (2005). Vocabulary visits: Virtual field trips for content vocabulary development. *The Reading Teacher, 59,* 262–268.

Callella, T., Sanoiloff, S., & Tom, D. (2001). *Making your word wall more interactive.* Huntington Beach, CA: Creative Teaching Press.

Campbell, D. & Halderman, K. (2004). *Word walls activities.* Westminster, CA: Teacher Created Resources.

Cooper, J. D., Chard, D. J., & Kiger, N. D. (2006). *The struggling reader.* New York: Scholastic.

Coyne, M. D., Simmons, D. C., & Kame'enui, E. J. (2004). Vocabulary instruction for young children at risk of experiencing reading difficulties: Teaching word meanings during shared storybook readings. In J. F. Baumann & E. J. Kame'enui (Eds.), *Vocabulary instruction: Research to practice* (pp. 41–58). New York: Guilford Press.

Ellermeyer, D. & Rowell, J. (2005). *Perfect poems for teaching sight words.* New York: Scholastic.

Hart, B. & Risley, T. R. (1995). *Meaningful differences in the everyday experiences of young American children: The everyday experience of one- and two-year-old American children.* Baltimore, MD: Paul H. Brookes.

Leslie, L. & Caldwell, J. (2001). *Qualitative reading inventory–3.* New York: Addison Wesley Longman.

Lubliner, S. (2005). *Getting into words.* Baltimore, MD: Paul H. Brookes.

Lynch, J. (2005). *Making word walls work.* New York: Scholastic.

National Reading Panel. (2000). *Report of the National Reading Panel: Teaching children to read. Report of the subgroups.* Washington, DC: U.S. Department of Health and Human Services, National Institutes of Health.

Nagy, W. E. (1988). *Teaching vocabulary to improve reading comprehension.* ERIC Clearinghouse on Reading and Communication Skills.

Reynolds, L. (2004). *Poems for sight word practice.* Peterborough, NH: Crystal Springs Books.

Richek, M. (2003). *Vocabulary strategies that boost your students' reading comprehension.* (Video). Seattle: Bureau of Education and Research.

Spann, M. B. (2001). *The Scholastic big book of word walls.* New York: Scholastic.

Wagstaff, J. (1999). *Teaching reading and writing with word walls.* New York: Scholastic.

White, T. G., Graves, M. F., & Slater, W. H. (1990). Growth of reading vocabulary in diverse elementary schools: Decoding and word meaning. *Journal of Educational Psychology, 82,* 281–290.

Williams, R. (2005). *Sight word poetry pages.* New York: Scholastic.

Chapter 4

Fluency

Classroom Snapshot

Justin is a third-grade reader in a remedial program. His instructional reading level is roughly equivalent to a beginning second grader. As he reads new material, he slowly and painstakingly sounds out words, and often goes back to reread. He pays little attention to punctuation marks and often reads past periods without stopping. Justin is usually several pages behind his classmates when reading in a group. When he is finished with a text, his comments during discussion and retellings indicate that he has understood some of what he has read but seems to miss the big ideas and how the story fits together. He also has misunderstood some key points because of mistakes involving punctuation.

It's obvious that Justin has some kind of reading problem. He's not making the progress his peers are, and his comprehension is spotty. His teacher gave him some phonics assessments (see Chapter 2) and found that he can apply phonics skills pretty well when reading isolated words, and he has a strong oral vocabulary. What is causing his difficulty?

Justin lacks fluency. He reads slowly, word by word. He doesn't group the words into meaningful phrases, and doesn't see how sentences go together. Because he ignores punctuation, he misunderstands who's talking in dialogue, and he reads so slowly that he can't put pieces of the sentences together to make a picture in his mind of what's going on.

This chapter will discuss the importance of fluency in reading. We will look at the relationship between fluency and the other components of phonics, vocabulary, and comprehension and the impact these elements have on the success of struggling readers like Justin.

We will discuss some ways to assess a reader's fluency, and look at research-supported instructional strategies for groups and individuals that you can use to boost your students' fluency in meaningful ways.

What Is Fluency?

Sometimes fluency is defined as the rate, or number of words per minute, at which a student reads. Speed is certainly an important factor, and one to keep an eye on, but fluency goes beyond that. Reading fluency also includes a child's ability to read smoothly, accurately, and with attention to punctuation and prosody (the use of appropriate pitch, stress, and phrasing). Fluent reading sounds like talking. It's smooth, without a lot of rereading, and it's fast enough so the sentences flow together, but not so fast that the sense of the sentence is lost. Punctuation is reflected in the reader's voice. There's expression, with some words in each sentence given a little more oomph. Fluent reading engages the listener.

A fifth-grade teacher recently commented to me about one of her students, "What's the big deal with fluency, anyway? She doesn't need to be a fluent reader unless she's going to be reading aloud to people, and how often do we do that?" Let's see what the big deal is.

Fluency and the Other Areas of Reading

Like my colleague, I used to think fluency was pretty unimportant. After all, lots of my students read silently, in their heads, and they seemed to understand perfectly well. But I began to notice some problems cropping up. Students with oral fluency problems were missing some of the details of the text. When we talked about who did what in the story, they had some confusion. And it took longer and longer for them to read the sections of text we were focusing on. I began to look a little closer.

Fluency was having a direct effect on my students' comprehension, and the lack of comprehension affected their ability to read with appropriate expression. If a child doesn't understand what is happening in a text, he or she cannot possibly read with the proper emphasis and phrasing. Students who do not use punctuation will just ignore paragraph and sentence breaks. The built-in structure of the text, the main ideas and details, are lost. My students didn't know who was talking in the story because they read right past periods, quotation marks, and paragraph breaks.

Research supports these observations. The NAEP 2002 *Special Study of Oral Reading* examined the oral reading of fourth-grade students across the United States. That study found that more fluent readers also demonstrated higher comprehension, and nonfluent readers scored lower in reading accuracy and comprehension. Students who performed at higher levels on the comprehension assessment were most likely to read with greater accuracy and at a faster rate in the oral reading study. Overall, the data from the study shows that accuracy, rate, fluency, and comprehension are all related.

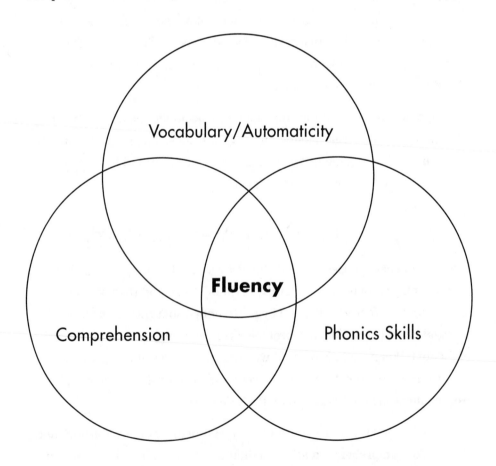

Fluency is impacted by phonics, vocabulary, and comprehension.

So students' comprehension of a text is often linked to their fluent reading of these texts. Poor word recognition skills and limited vocabulary knowledge can also cause problems with fluency. As the *Report from the National Reading Panel* states, "High-speed word recognition frees a reader's cognitive resources so that the meaning of a text can be the focus of attention" (p. 3-6). Similarly, difficulty with word recognition slows down the reading process and takes up valuable mental resources that are necessary for comprehension. If a student reads very slowly or makes many "backtracks" and corrections, the sense of the sentence, paragraph, and even the whole page can be undermined, and comprehension is lost, because the reader's focus is on figuring out the individual words, rather than the larger meaning of the text.

If a child can decode words quickly, he or she will tend to be more fluent. A child with good ability to quickly recall letter patterns and chunks will read the whole text faster. In our classroom snapshot, Justin's reading is slow and laborious. He's spending so much time on difficult words that he can't think about the meaning of the sentences. Although the teacher found that Justin can decode isolated words, he's going to need some faster decoding strategies (see chapters 2 and 3) as well as fluency instruction. His frequent rereading of sentences and difficult words makes the ideas very fragmented, so it's hard to get the big idea. He can't use prediction effectively, since he's missing the meaning. A visual representation of the role of fluency with the other pieces of reading is shown on the previous page.

The fluent reader can perform multiple tasks, such as word recognition and comprehension, at the same time. If you are fluent, you can quickly group words into meaningful grammatical units. You pay attention to punctuation and quickly determine where to place emphasis and when to pause to convey meaning. For example, the following sentences have a completely different meaning depending on which word is emphasized:

> **I** didn't say you took the cookie.
> (Someone else might have said you took it.)

> I didn't say you took the **cookie**.
> (Maybe you took something else.)

DEVELOPMENT OF FLUENCY

How does fluency develop? A major factor is having a good model of fluent reading, someone who reads to the child. When children don't have a good model of what a fluent reader sounds like, they may often think reading is saying every word slowly and carefully, because that's what they hear from their classmates, and even their parents or teachers. Sometimes we get so caught up with reading a text accurately, we forget to make it sound like we're talking.

Another key is experience with reading. As with any other skill, practice improves performance. As children read more, pieces of the process become automatic. They begin to recognize some words immediately. Other words are decoded quickly and automatically.

In a ten-minute sustained silent reading time, a fluent reader can read ten times the amount of text as a struggling reader. In today's curriculum-crowded elementary schools, many struggling readers simply don't have the time to finish reading an assigned text. Some students have learned to "fake-read," watching their peers and turning a page at the same time as the more fluent readers do, whether they've read the text or not. It's not about getting the meaning of the text for these students, it's about finishing it.

Why Some Students Are Fluent and Some Aren't

Hypotheses by Richard Allington (1983):

● Fluent children have fluent models.

● Successful readers can focus on expression while poor readers are focusing on word recognition and phonics application.

● Fluent readers get more opportunities to read.

● Fluent readers are often reading at their instructional or independent level. Struggling readers are often reading at their frustration level.

● Fluent readers understand the goal of reading is to make meaning rather than to only pronounce words accurately.

ASSESS

How do you know if your students are fluent readers? There are a variety of ways to assess fluency. The key is to listen closely to how your students read aloud, looking at their speed, smoothness, accuracy, and attention to punctuation and prosody.

Timed Reading Assessments

A good place to begin is with a one-minute timed reading, an informal way to gain a picture of a child's reading. You can use text from your basal reading program, leveled books, an informal reading inventory, or leveled, numbered texts from commercial programs such as Read Naturally, DIBELS, or Reading A–Z (see others listed on page 144). Just be sure the student has not read it previously.

ONE-MINUTE TIMED READING

Procedure

1. Select a new, previously unseen text at your student's expected instructional reading level (between 90 percent to 95 percent accuracy). (See Chapter 1 for more information on how to determine instructional level.)

2. Make a copy of the passage to use as a recording sheet for each student you assess. If the words aren't already numbered, add numbers at the end of each line for easy scoring.

3. Give a brief introduction to the text.

4. Ask the student to read aloud for one minute. Follow along on a copy of the text and mark any errors the student makes. Errors include omissions, substitutions, mispronunciations, and words you tell the child after waiting for three seconds. Repetitions are not counted as errors, nor are any errors the student corrects. Simply put a slash through words to indicate errors.

5. At the end of one minute, stop the student, and calculate the number of words he or she has read correctly by subtracting the number of errors from the total words read (see below).

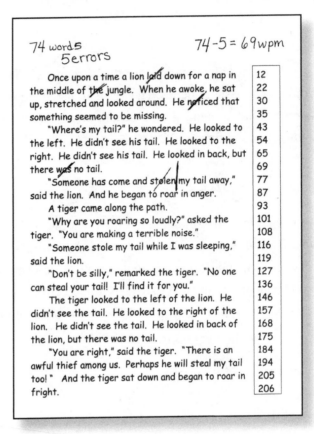

A second grader's timed reading sample

This second-grade student read 74 words in one minute, with five errors, for a score of 69 words per minute. He seems to be reading with enough speed to be able to focus on meaning, but is he on track? Let's take a look at normal ranges for rate of reading, by grade level.

HOW FAST IS FAST ENOUGH?

How do you know when a student is reading at an appropriate speed? Many researchers have looked at normal ranges (Rasinski, 2003). Some school districts have set their own target rates, as have some states. Those shown on page 131 seem to be appropriate targets. These come from Jan Hasbrouck and Gerald A. Tindal's work in 2006.

Oral Reading Fluency Norm Rates

Grade	Fall WCPM*	Winter WCPM	Spring WCPM
1	—	—	60
2	53	78	94
3	79	93	114
4	99	112	118
5	105	118	128
6	115	132	145
7	147	158	167
8	156	167	171

*WCPM—Words Correct Per Minute

The second-grade child, whose timed-reading sample is shown on page 130 would be reading faster than what a teacher might expect of a student at the beginning of the year. Her rate reflects where she should be at midyear.

Because sight word knowledge and decoding skills are such strong contributors to fluency, assessments of those areas are also useful for determining appropriate instructional focus, especially if the student is reading very slowly. It may be that the student really understands fluency but needs help with phonics or vocabulary. (See chapters 2 and 3.)

Beyond Speed: Fluency Scales

After giving a timed reading to determine rate, the next step is to look closer at the child's actual reading performance, to see how he or she expresses meaning by grouping words and using expression and intonation. There are two types of scales to use for this: the Holistic Oral Reading Fluency Scale, which gives one score reflecting speed, phrasing, and expression (page 133), and the Multidimensional Fluency Scale, which gives separate scores for expression, phrasing, smoothness, and pace (page 134).

Lack of Sight Word Knowledge Rx

It is tempting to provide isolated drills on sight words when fluency is poor. However, drilling out of context rarely transfers into an improvement in reading running text. Reading phrases or sentences with sight words included is a more meaning-centered and effective way to teach these common words. See Chapter 3 for a discussion of sight words and descriptions of appropriate activities to help readers build their sight word vocabulary.

THE HOLISTIC AND MULTIDIMENSIONAL SCALES

Using the holistic fluency scale is quicker, but the multidimensional scale gives the most complete reflection of a child's oral fluency skills. For struggling readers, the multidimensional scale will provide you with the most information for determining appropriate instruction. For the bulk of a class, the holistic scale gives enough information to plan teaching steps. Both scales are used the same way.

Procedure

1. Select a passage at each student's instructional reading level (an expected 90 percent to 95 percent accuracy) and make one copy to use as a recording sheet for each student you assess.

2. Allow the student to practice the selection one time.

3. Ask the student to read the passage orally. Mark the phrasing by placing slashes (/) to indicate where the student pauses between words. Circle any ignored punctuation.

4. Rate the student holistically or on each dimension of the fluency scale.

Once/upon/a time/a lion/laid/down/for a nap/in	12
the middle/of the jungle/ When he/awoke/he sat/	22
up,/stretched/and looked/around⊙ He/noticed that/	30
something/seemed/to be missing.	35
"Where's my tail?"/he/~~wondered.~~/He looked/to	43
the left⊙ He/didn't see his/tail⊙ He looked/to the	54
right./ He didn't/see his tail. He looked/in back⊙but/	65
there was/no tail.	69
"Someone/ has come/and stolen/my tail away⊙"	77
said the lion./ And he/began to roar/in anger. //Stop.	87
A tiger came along the path.	93
"Why are you roaring so loudly?" asked the	101
tiger. "You are making a terrible noise."	108
"Someone stole my tail while I was sleeping,"	116
said the lion.	119
"Don't be silly," remarked the tiger. "No one	127
can steal your tail! I'll find it for you."	136
The tiger looked to the left of the lion. He	146
didn't see the tail. He looked to the right of the	157
lion. He didn't see the tail. He looked in back of	168
the lion, but there was no tail.	175
"You are right," said the tiger. "There is an	184
awful thief among us. Perhaps he will steal my tail	194
too!" And the tiger sat down and began to roar in	205
fright.	206

A second grader's timed reading scored for phrasing

Holistic Oral Reading Fluency Scale

4 Reads primarily in larger, meaningful phrase groups. Although the reader may occasionally repeat a phrase or make and correct an error, these do not detract from the overall structure of the story. Preservation of the author's syntax is consistent. Some or most of the story is read with expression. Reads at an appropriate rate.

3 Reads primarily in three- and four-word phrase groups with a few smaller groupings. However, the majority of phrasing seems appropriate and preserves the syntax of the author. Reader attempts to read expressively. Generally reads at an appropriate rate.

2 Reads primarily in two-word phrase groups with some three- and four-word groupings. Some word-by-word reading may be present. Word groupings may seem awkward and unrelated to the larger context of the sentence or passage. Very little of the text is read with expression. Reads significant sections of the text excessively slowly or fast.

1 Reads primarily word by word. Occasional two- or three-word phrases may occur—but these are infrequent and/or they do not preserve meaningful syntax. Lacks expressive interpretation. Reads text excessively slowly.

A score of 1 should also be given to a student who reads with excessive speed, ignoring punctuation and other phrase boundaries, and reads with little or no expression.

This version adapted by T. V. Rasinski in *Assessing Reading Fluency*, 2004, Pacific Resources for Education and Learning Honolulu, HI. Available at: http://www.prel.org/programs/rel/re.asp. Original rubric from *Listening to Children Read Aloud: Oral Fluency* by G. S. Pinnell, J. J. Pikulski, K. K. Wixson, J. R. Campbell, P. B. Gough, & A. S. Beatty, 1995, Washington, D. C.: U.S. Department of Education, National Center for education Statistics. Available at: http://nces.ed.gov/pubs95/web/95762.asp.

MULTIDIMENSIONAL FLUENCY SCALE

Dimension	1	2	3	4
A. Expression and Volume _____ Score	Reads with little expression or enthusiasm in voice. Reads words as if simply to get them out. Little sense of trying to make text sound like natural language. Tends to read in a quiet voice.	Some expression. Begins to use voice to make text sound like natural language in some areas, but not others. Focus remains largely on saying the words. Still reads in a quiet voice.	Sounds like natural language throughout the better part of the passage. Occasionally slips into expressionless reading. Voice volume is generally appropriate throughout the text.	Reads with good expression and enthusiasm throughout the text. Sounds like natural language. The reader is able to vary expression and volume to match his/her interpretation of the passage.
B. Phrasing _____ Score	Monotonic with little sense of phrase boundaries; frequent word-by-word reading.	Frequent two- and three-word phrases giving the impression of choppy reading; improper stress and intonation that fail to mark ends of sentences and clauses.	Mixture of run-ons, mid-sentence pauses for breath, and possibly some choppiness; reasonable stress/intonation.	Generally well phrased, mostly in clause and sentence units, with adequate attention to expression.
C. Smoothness _____ Score	Frequent extended pauses, hesitations, false starts, sound-outs, repetitions, and/or multiple attempts.	Several "rough spots" in text where extended pauses, hesitations, etc., are more frequent and disruptive.	Occasional breaks in smoothness caused by difficulties with specific words and/or structures.	Generally smooth reading with some breaks, but word and structure difficulties are resolved quickly, usually through self-correction.
D. Pace (during sections of minimal disruption) _____ Score	Slow and laborious or extremely fast.	Moderately slow.	Uneven mixture of fast and slow reading.	Consistently conversational.
Total score _____	Generally, total scores below 8 indicate that fluency may be a concern. Scores of 8 or above indicate that the student is making good progress in fluency.			

This version adapted by T. V. Rasinski in *Assessing Reading Fluency*, 2004, Pacific Resources for Education and Learning Honolulu, HI. Available at: http://www.prel.org/programs/ rel/re.asp. Original rubric from "Training Teachers to Attend to Their Students' Oral Reading Fluency" by J. Zutell and T. V. Rasinski, 1991, *Theory Into Practice*, 30, pp. 211–217.

The assessment on page 132 shows that the second-grade student began haltingly, with a lot of word-by-word reading. (The slashes between words indicate pauses.) The student also ignored some periods, resulting in running some sentences together. As the student read on, he began to group some words into two- or three-word phrases. His phrasing did not always fit the intended meaning, as when he read, "He looked/in back but/ there was/no tail." He continued to ignore ending punctuation in several cases. He read 87 words in one minute, with one error (*wondered*). There were longer pauses before the words *noticed* and *wondered* as he tried to work them out. The reading is fast enough when measured in words per minute, but it is also choppy and lacking expression for most of the text. Using the holistic scale on page 133, I would give his reading a score of 2, noting that speed was not really an issue to address.

On the multidimensional scale on page 134, I would score the same reading 1 for both dimensions of expression and phrasing, a 2 for smoothness, and a 3 for pace. I can see that this student needs help with phrasing and using expression, especially with dialogue. He doesn't need to read faster. Added together, the student's score would total 7, indicating that fluency is a concern.

Beginning in second grade, formal fluency assessment is appropriate at the beginning, middle, and end of the year. I don't formally assess first graders until the end of the year. Any students who are struggling with fluency may be assessed every three or four weeks. You can also informally assess your students' fluency every few weeks by listening to a page or two of a text they are reading during self-selected reading time or guided reading groups. Many of the activities described later in the chapter will also provide you with information to make further decisions about your students' progress in this important area.

2 | Reads primarily in two-word phrase groups with some three- and four-word groupings. Some word-by-word reading may be present. Word groupings may seem awkward and unrelated to the larger context of the sentence or passage. Very little of the text is read with expression. Reads significant sections of the text excessively slowly or fast.

SEE PAGE 133

Dimension	
A. Expression and Volume	
Score	1
B. Phrasing	
Score	1
C. Smoothness	
Score	2
D. Pace (during sections of minimal disruption)	
Score	3
Total score	7

SEE PAGE 134

Both fluency scales indicate that this reader needs support with expression, phrasing, and smoothness.

PLAN

Once you've had a chance to assess students' fluency, you are ready to design some lessons. The students whose reading we evaluated on pages 130 and 132 do not need to work on rate, based on their assessments. Given the information we got from the multidimensional fluency scale for the student on page 132, we would need to design instruction to develop this student's ability to read with expression and correct phrasing. If your students need help with speed, you might try some timed readings with feedback on an individual basis. If you have a group of students who read fast enough, but whose reading is too choppy and word-by-word, you will want to plan different lessons. The chart below gives some suggested activities for different problems you may discover through your assessments. The rest of this chapter will describe these activities and how to use them in your classroom.

If the child . . .	Then you might try . . .	Page number
reads very slowly, but accurately	Shared Reading: Fluency Focus	139
	Partner Reading With Feedback	143
	Readers Theater	145
reads too fast	Provide a Model: Fluency	137
	Shared Reading: Fluency Focus	139
	Score It!	141
	Partner Reading With Feedback	142
	Readers Theater	145
reads word by word	Provide a Model: Fluency	137
	Shared Reading: Fluency Focus	139
	Reread Easy and/or Familiar Text	140
ignores punctuation	Provide a Model: Fluency	137
	Shared Reading: Fluency Focus	139
	Add an Emphasis to Punctuation	147
lacks expression	Provide a Model: Fluency	137
	Shared Reading: Fluency Focus	139
	Score It!	141
	Partner Reading With Feedback	142
	Readers Theater	145
lacks smoothness with many errors and self-corrections	Shared Reading: Fluency Focus	139
	Reread Easy and/or Familiar Text	140
fails to make progress after fluency instruction	Intense Intervention	148

TEACH

The good news is that children's fluency often improves rapidly with good instruction. What kinds of things should you do to support your struggling readers? There's lots of research to support classroom activities that involve practicing oral reading with feedback and guidance to target specific areas of fluency development.

The National Reading Panel found that students need frequent opportunities for repeated reading and other procedures in which they read passages orally multiple times while receiving guidance or feedback from peers, parents, or teachers, and that such experiences improve fluency, word knowledge, and even comprehension. These procedures help improve students' reading ability at least through fifth grade, and improve the reading of students with learning problems much later than this (p. 3-20).

What will it look like in the classroom? You may work on fluency with your whole class at one time, in a small reading group, or with individual students. Large group activities, such as a mini-lesson on reading dialogue with expression and phrasing, can fit into your day at many different times. Fluency practice can be a great warm-up for other lessons, an effective transition between recesses and other lessons, or a fun way to begin or end your day together. You can use science or social studies material for shared or modeled reading and even for Readers Theater.

Small-group activities fit easily into your guided reading group time. Fluency practice is one more way to flexibly group those students who need practice in the different areas of the scoring scales. Individual instruction can occur during self-selected reading time, centers, or other times during the day. Many of the following activities can be used with a variety of group sizes, and either hetero- or homogeneous groupings. Let's see how your classroom might look during fluency work.

PROVIDE A MODEL: FLUENCY (Large or small group, individual)

Read to your students every day. One of the easiest but most powerful ways to help students see what fluency is all about is to provide a model of fluent reading. As Richard Allington (1983) theorized, fluent readers understand what the target is. Sadly, for many of our students today, the once common ritual of a bedtime story is not part of their family culture. For too many students, the opportunity to hear a fluent reader happens only at school. And often, an overcrowded curriculum or a focus on test preparation has pushed oral reading by the teacher into the "extras" category. Children today don't always have someone to read to them.

Children, especially struggling readers, need to have that model of what fluent reading sounds like. This can include books on tape, books read by peers, and, most important, a daily read-aloud by the teacher. When you read aloud, you send a powerful message that meaning is carried by the way we group words together and emphasize certain words, not just the words themselves.

During an oral reading experience, you can do a lot to model fluency for students.

- As you read, occasionally stop to highlight aspects of fluent reading. Discuss for example, how you read the dialogue as you think a character might say it, and how your voice goes up or down with sentence structure. Ask students to repeat a phrase or sentence the way you say it. For example, you might say, "I think Father Bear must be angry that someone has been in his chair, but Baby Bear must feel very sad when he sees his chair broken. Listen how I try to show how they feel in the way I say their words."

- Model and help students notice how different stresses change the meaning of sentences, like so: "Do you think Father Bear is upset that someone has been sitting in the chair, or the fact that it's *his* chair? I'll say it two different ways and you see what sounds better: Someone's been *sitting* in my chair. . . . Someone's been sitting in *my* chair."

- Occasionally interrupt your reading to show how you could read something more fluently, saying something like, "I don't think I said that quite right. Let me try it again." When you do this, you are also modeling self-monitoring, an important skill for comprehension.

While reading aloud to students tends to be more common at the primary grades, it is an effective and important tool with older students, as well. It helps students at all levels see how reading is emotionally powerful and motivating. For your students who struggle and read word by word,

A Word of Caution

It's important that you don't interrupt the story too much to do this kind of work—especially during a first reading. The flow of expressive reading helps students create meaning and shouldn't be interrupted. Pointing out fluent elements of your reading is an effective technique during a second or third reading of a text.

it can show them that reading is actually an enjoyable activity that might be worth a little work to achieve. You can help students explore a variety of genres and material that may be above their own reading levels through well-chosen read-alouds.

Another important benefit of read-alouds is the opportunity to develop a wide range of vocabulary and needed background information for fluent reading of independent and instructional reading materials. Again, students benefit when you stop occasionally or follow up the reading to discuss interesting words and their meanings: "I think porridge must be some kind of hot cereal, like oatmeal, don't you? It has to cool off, and they are going to eat it with a spoon. Let's see if that makes sense."

See Chapter 3 for more on "harvesting" interesting vocabulary words from read-alouds.

SHARED READING: FLUENCY FOCUS
(Large or small group)

Many students never physically get a feel for what fluent reading is. They continually "voice-point," or read word by word, in a monotone. Shared reading is one way for students to safely experience what fluent reading is like. During shared reading, students read a text together and at the same time hear the fluent reading of the text being read by those around them. For some students, even if they aren't actually reading aloud, they benefit from being surrounded by great examples of fluency. Soon they'll be chiming in, as well.

- Place a big book or large chart in a place where everyone can see it. You can also use an overhead or distribute copies of text. I prefer a big chart or book, so I can watch students' eyes and provide a model of tracking as I move my hand over the words.

- Read the text aloud the first time, using good expression and phrasing, and then invite students to read the text in unison. Provide students with coaching and feedback on stress, pitch, and emphasis. You can try reading it in many different ways, like this: "Let's read the poem this time like we love the leaves falling. See how nice our voices sound. It's relaxed and gentle. . . . This time, let's read it as if we are not looking forward to having to rake the leaves. We'll have to be louder and rougher. What words will we need to punch up and say stronger?"

Shared reading activities work extremely well because the text is modeled and it becomes familiar with repetition, leaving students free to focus on phrasing and meaning, rather than decoding. They can really focus on making it sound like talking. You may repeat a text three or four times in a single sitting, and then return to the text the following day.

There are many appropriate texts and methods for shared reading. For example, poetry is an excellent vehicle for shared reading, with its built-in rhythm. You can read a poem completely in unison, or students can be divided into groups to read different sections. You can write poems on sentence strips, chart paper, or an overhead transparency using several different colors, with individuals or groups of students reading each stanza or selected lines. Books such as *Joyful Noise: Poems for Two Voices* by Paul Fleischman and Mary Ann Hoberman's *You Read to Me, I'll Read to You* series are already divided into sections.

Shared reading has traditionally been done in the primary grades, but has been shown to be effective with all age levels. *On the Same Page: Shared Reading Beyond the Primary Grades*, by Janet Allen (2002), is an excellent resource for middle-grade teachers. She demonstrates how to use shared reading in the content areas, as well.

REREAD EASY AND/OR FAMILIAR TEXT
(Large or small group, individual)

Part of the reason students lack fluency in reading is the difficulty they have with the vocabulary and decoding challenges of new text. For that reason, practicing texts where the words have already been decoded and the vocabulary worked out allows students to focus on meaning and fluency. The model for Marie Clay's Reading Recovery intervention for the most at-risk first-grade students employs rereading of familiar storybooks as a vital component.

Early-grade teachers often begin guided reading lessons with a brief rereading of familiar texts. You can provide students with book boxes that hold a variety of previously read texts for practice during independent seat work or partner reading sessions. Poetry journals, where poems used previously as shared reading materials are collected for rereading, also work very well. Whichever materials you select, rereading previously read material has been shown to have a positive effect on word recognition, vocabulary comprehension, and fluency. Practice not only leads to improvements in reading the familiar text, but transfers to new passages as well (*Report of the National Reading Panel*, pp. 3-18–3-20).

For some older students, providing them with an authentic purpose for reading easy material is very effective. At my school, as at many others, older students are paired as reading buddies with younger students, giving the older students an opportunity to read to beginning readers. Fourth graders may meet with first graders once a week for the whole year, to share a good book. The older student picks a book from the library or the classroom collection of picture books and practices it several times until he or she is ready to read it fluently to the young buddy. Students meet up in the classroom or hall during designated buddy time and read. Sometimes the younger student has also practiced a book to read to the older buddy. Everyone benefits. No stigma is attached to the reading of the "easy books" because it is done for the benefit of the younger students. Older readers also benefit by developing greater fluency.

SCORE IT! (Large or small group)

Just as you may use a scoring guide, or rubric, to discuss and improve students' writing, you can introduce a set of criteria that students can use to judge their own and others' reading. This process helps students understand exactly what you are talking about when you discuss reading fluently.

● Either present a scoring guide that you've made, showing students how to use each scoring item, or develop a scoring guide as a class. When my students and I develop the scoring guide together, I find the best result if I have a target in mind, and then I demonstrate both fluent and nonfluent reading. The students key into the difference in quality of the readings and then help me put the characteristics of fluent reading into their language. For example, I might first read a selection in a monotone, and then again with expression, and ask what was different. I do the same thing with stopping at periods and phrasing—the first time I don't stop at periods and I take breaths in the middle of a phrase. The next time I read, I pay attention to the phrasing and punctuation. A rubric that a group of third graders developed appears on page 142.

● Once after students have developed and/or used the rubric, use the language over and over with them. For example, you might say, "Listen to me read this section, and see if I'm grouping my words so you understand the sentence." Or, "Let's read this poem and try to be very smooth in our reading." The more students are aware of the scoring guide, the more likely they are to consider it in their reading.

Student Fluency Rubric

	Needs work	Okay	Great
I stop at periods and other punctuation marks.			
I group my words together so the reading makes sense.			
I don't read too fast or too slow—I'm just right.			
I fix my mistakes quickly.			
My reading is smooth.			
My reading is fun to listen to.			

For some students, having a tape recording of their oral reading and listening to themselves is a powerful tool. It can become even more powerful when you use the scoring guide to focus their attention.

PARTNER READING WITH FEEDBACK
(Small group or individual)

Repeated reading with feedback has been shown to be an effective combination for increasing fluency with students who read quickly and without expression—and for motivating them to reread familiar texts. While ideally a highly qualified teacher would give input, peer partners can also be trained to give useful feedback to readers. Students often seem to be more motivated when reading with a partner or when there is a stopwatch involved. Both of these elements make reading-partner "trains" a big hit.

For reading trains, students select a text that they have read at least once. (It's a great time to practice reading a book they will later read to their younger buddies.) Then the trains are ready to roll.

● Have students pair up, with one child reading and the other listening.

- Set a timer for 1 or 1½ minutes.

- Students read until the timer goes off.

- At the end of the time, the reader places a sticky note or piece of colored tape to show where he or she ended.

- Listeners give positive feedback to readers, using the language of the oral fluency rubric used in class.

- Readers switch to another partner and reread the same passage, starting in the same place that they did last time.

- At the end of the time, readers compare how far they read compared to their first timing and get feedback from their new partners.

- This process can be repeated several more times, or the partners can switch, with the original listener doing the reading this time.

Giving positive fluency feedback is like any other skill students learn. It must be modeled for students to be successful. Before asking students to give feedback, be sure to role-play positive responses that use the common language of the rubric. In the context of a safe and caring classroom, both the reader and the listener benefit. Readers get practice, and listeners get the chance to think hard about the components of fluent reading.

Self-Monitoring

For many students, keeping a graph to show improvement in the number of words correctly read in a timed reading is very motivating. There's something very exciting about seeing the numbers go up. I've found this especially effective for students who are adequate readers, but just don't seem to care much about reading accurately at an appropriate pace. Here's how it works.

- Pick out a fairly short, unfamiliar passage. Choose any genre, although nonfiction or poetry can be very motivating for this type of reluctant reader.

- Ask the student to read the selection aloud while you record errors and the number of words read correctly, just as in the words-per-minute assessment (page 129).

- Record the resulting score on a bar graph (see page 144).

- Provide a good model by reading the whole selection to the student.

- Ask the student to practice, with help or independently, several times. Some commercial programs, like Read Naturally (see box below), provide taped or computer- based models for students to listen to as they read along.

- Your feedback is important during this phase. You can help with the more difficult words, ask the child to practice a particularly tricky section, and provide tips on reading the punctuation.

- After the student feels comfortable with the text, do a second timed reading and record the resulting score on the same graph. Most students respond positively to seeing the numbers increase. For students who enjoy a little bit of competition, this can be very motivating as they work to get their graphs higher than the time before.

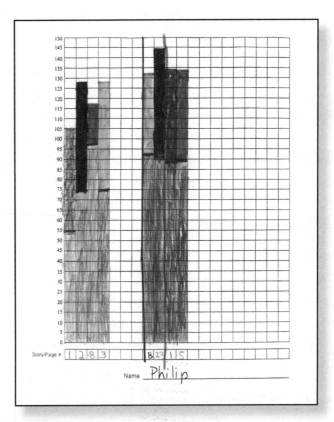

A fifth grader's graph comparing words per minute of first and subsequent readings of several different pages and texts.

Commercial Programs

Read Naturally
(readnaturally.com)

Quickreads
(Pearsonlearning.com)

Reading Fluency Coach
(sfcatalog.pearson.com)

Reading Tutors
(Reading-tutors.com)

A note of caution: When you are doing this activity, make sure that students realize that reading quickly is not the only important aspect of fluency. Too much emphasis on speed can result in students losing comprehension as they rush through a selection.

READERS THEATER (Small group)

My students often request that we "read it again like a play" right after we've read a short text. We love to perform our text. Readers Theater is the dramatic oral reading of a script or other text. Generally, no props, costumes, or movements are involved. The only way to convey meaning is through the reader's voice. In order to accomplish this, the students have to do a lot of practice. So Readers Theater is an authentic and motivating reason to do repeated readings.

Research supports Readers Theater as a powerful tool for fluency improvement, and studies have also demonstrated a very positive impact on both comprehension and vocabulary (Griffith & Rasinski, 2004).

There are several ways to implement Readers Theater in your classroom. Many books at the early reading level lend themselves to Readers Theater just as they are, with one child doing the narrative parts and others reading the dialogue of an assigned character. You might photocopy and mark sections students will read from, as shown below. Or you may have students use highlighting tape or erasable markers that can be used right in the book to show which part is read by each participant (see the example on page 146). This procedure can be implemented easily, and provides another reason to do a reread of familiar text.

Narrator: Rushing up to the top level, I get seats near the front.

~~Aunt Pam joins me.~~ "Honey, put on your baseball cap, your sunglasses and suntan lotion. Don't forget that we promised your mom that we'd make up a scrapbook of this trip. Your camera, notepad and pen are in your knapsack."

Narrator: I was hoping that she'd forgotten about the scrapbook.

"Tomorrow," ~~Aunt Pam says,~~ "we'll have a chance to see some places up close. Today we'll have an overview."

~~I scratch at my arm again.~~ "And when we get back to the apartment, I mean flat, can we go to a drugstore and get some bug bite spray?"

~~She nods.~~ "Remind me. Sometimes aunts forget."

~~I grin at her.~~

~~She grins back.~~ "You know, I just love doing things with you. It's so nice when you

42

A copy of a page from *You Can't Eat Your Chicken Pox, Amber Brown* marked for Readers Theater: Speaker tags and unneeded text have been crossed out in the running copy, the narrator's part has been marked script-style in the left margin, and Aunt Pam's part has been highlighted.

> "I'm hungry," said Baby Bear. "I want some porridge."
>
> "The porridge is too hot," said Mother Bear. "We must let it cool."
>
> So the three bears went for a walk.

You can also use highlighting tape to mark a speaking part directly on the page.

Resources for Readers Theater Scripts

www.teachingheart.net/readerstheater.htm

www.readinga-z.com (click through the Fluency tab or go directly to www.readinga-z.com/fluency/scripts.html)

www.aaronshep.com (click through to author Aaron Shephard's "RT Page" or go directly to www.aaronshep.com/rt/index.html)

www.readinglady.com (click through downloads and select Readers Theater)

Fall Is Fabulous: Readers Theater Scripts and Extended Activities by L. Blau

Readers Theater, Grade 3, by Evan-Moore Publishers

Readers Theater for Building Fluency by J. Worthy

Stories on Stage by A. Shepard

Tadpole Tales and Other Totally Terrific Treats for Readers Theater by A. Frederick

Texts for Fluency Practice by T. Rasinski & L. Griffith

Short sections of longer text can also be converted into Readers Theater in the same manner. Often, simply determining which character is actually speaking the lines is an excellent lesson for comprehension. Unneeded text, such as "he said," can simply be deleted.

Sources for ready-to-go scripts are becoming abundant. There are many scripts available on the Internet (see list at left) and in book collections. You can also create your own scripts, or have students rewrite a text they have read into a script. Science and social studies content can be powerfully conveyed through a Readers Theater script.

When using scripts, several procedures can increase students' abilities to read fluently and comprehend well.

- Hand out scripts with one character's part highlighted on each script.

- Provide an oral model by reading the text to students as they follow along, pausing to discuss the ideas.

- Read the scripts together several times. Have an individual child or partners read each part. Then switch parts, and have each child or pair read a different part.

- Provide coaching and modeling to students on how to use their voices to convey meaning for the various parts. Brainstorm ideas with the class. "How would the prince say that if he was very angry? Let's all try it together."

- Negotiate and assign parts for the real performance.

- Practice the assigned parts.

- Perform for an audience.

For many students, the chance to perform can be extremely motivating. For others, it can be a nightmare. For reticent students, having a partner read the text with them can help relieve their anxiety. Sometimes just having heard the text read by another student is helpful. Wearing a hat, headband, or a simple mask can also help students feel distanced enough to make the reading less intimidating.

The performances do not have to be fancy or lengthy. The important thing is to provide an authentic purpose for rereading text with an eye toward fluency.

ADD AN EMPHASIS TO PUNCTUATION
(Large or small group, individual)

For those students who are reading right through the ending punctuation, here are two engaging activities that really emphasize the role of those marks.

Activity 1

- Write out the alphabet or a counting sequence, inserting various punctuation, as shown below.

  > 123? 4567! 8910.

  > ABC? DE. F! GH! IJK? LM. NO. P,Q,R,S and T? UV–WX? Y. Z!

- Ask students to read the selection with expression. It's fun to move the marks around and read it again, or read it as a dialogue between two or more students.

Activity 2

- For students who need extra attention drawn toward punctuation, change the activity above by asking students to add body movements for each kind of punctuation. Students can clap hands for a period, stomp their feet for an exclamation point, put one hand in the air for a question, and put a hand to their mouths for each section of quotation marks, as if they were shouting. Your class will come up with favorite motions.

● Highlight the various punctuation marks with colored tape or markers before adding the motions. Often, a few experiences with this activity can be very beneficial. If children need extra help, you can silently make the appropriate motions to help them get back on track.

INTENSE INTERVENTION (Small group or individual)

For some struggling students, none of the above strategies will be enough. It may be that their reading level is too far below that of the rest of their classmates, or they do not get involved enough in larger-group shared reading. If after doing the above activities you are not seeing much improvement in speed, phrasing, expression, and smoothness, these students may need very direct instruction and modeling. A more intense fluency-development lesson combining modeling, shared reading, repeated reading, and feedback has been developed by Timothy Rasinski (2003). This intense practice can help those really struggling readers finally know what it feels like to read with fluency. Here is the procedure.

● Introduce a new short text and read it to your students while they follow along on their own copies.

● Discuss the meaning of the text with students.

● Read the passage together as a shared reading several times.

● Ask pairs of students to practice reading the text.

● Arrange for individuals or groups of students to perform the text to the class.

● Have students take a copy of the passage home for practice.

● The next day, have students reread the passage to you or a partner.

Poetry works especially well for this activity, but a small section of a story or nonfiction text will work, too. It depends what interests and motivates the students. You can also write specific text for students, using a language experience approach to ensure that the language structures are appropriate (see page 200). I especially recommend writing text together for your most struggling readers or students with very little knowledge of English.

I have found that this intense activity will probably only need to be done four or five times before you begin to see a lot of improvement in students' fluency.

Final Thoughts

As the year progresses, you can informally assess students according to the dimensions of the holistic and multidimensional fluency scales or the rubric you have developed. Much of the informal assessment can be done during regular reading groups or as you roam the classroom during independent reading times and listen to students read orally. You may need to give more frequent and formalized assessments, perhaps once a month, to your struggling readers to continually refine your instructional focus for them. (Remember that words-per-minute target rates increase through the year, as does the difficulty of the expected text.) Students who have already met target goals only need to be checked once per term, to make sure that they are still on track.

Fluency instruction can fit into your reading program in a variety of ways. Spending a few minutes a day with the whole class doing some shared reading, modeling read-alouds, having students reread familiar and easy material, and supporting students during individual practice or Readers Theater will be time well spent. Flexible groups can work with shared reading or intense fluency lessons. Try to keep the practice as enjoyable and meaningful as possible; fluent readers are engaged readers.

In the next chapter, we will focus on making sure that your fluent readers are understanding what they read, and offer some methods for developing comprehension strategies.

Further Reading and References

Allen, J. (2002). *On the same page: Shared reading beyond the primary grades.* Portland, ME: Stenhouse.

Allington, R. (1983). Fluency: The neglected goal of the reading program. *The Reading Teacher, 36,* 556–561.

Blau, L. (1997). *Fall Is fabulous: Readers Theater scripts and extended activities.* One From the Heart.

Blevins, W. (2001). *Building fluency: lessons and strategies for reading success.* New York: Scholastic.

Frederick, A. (1997). *Tadpole tales and other totally terrific treats for Readers Theater.* Portsmouth, NH: Teacher Ideas Press.

Griffith, L. W. & Rasinski, T. (2004). A focus on fluency: How one teacher incorporated fluency with her reading curriculum. *The Reading Teacher, 58*, 126–137.

Hasbrouck, J. &. Tindal, G. A. (2006). Oral reading fluency norms: A valuable assessment tool for reading teachers. *The Reading Teacher, 59*, 636–644.

Martinez, M., Roser, N., & Strecker, S. (1999). "I never thought I could be a star": A Readers Theater ticket to reading fluency. *The Reading Teacher, 52*, 326–334.

National Reading Panel. (2000). *Report of the National Reading Panel: Teaching children to read. Report of the subgroups.* Washington, DC: U.S. Department of Health and Human Services, National Institutes of Health.

Rasinski, T. V. (2003). *The fluent reader.* New York: Scholastic.

Rasinski, T. V. & Griffith, L. (2005). *Texts for fluency practice.* Huntington Beach, CA: Shell Educational Publishing.

Readers Theater, grade 3. (2003). Monterey, CA: Evan-Moore Publishers.

Shepard, A. (2005). *Stories on stage.* Olympia, WA: Shepard Publications.

Worthy, J. (2005). *Readers Theater for building fluency.* New York: Scholastic.

Chapter 5

Comprehension

Classroom Snapshot

Second-grader Bessie is reading a short text aloud to me. Her accuracy is good and she's using lots of expression. I'm pleased. Obviously, this text I've selected is well within her instructional level. As she finishes and sets the book aside, I ask her to tell me about what she's read. There's a long pause.

"Well, there was a girl," she begins slowly. "And a dad and a mom. I think they were going to go somewhere. But I'm not really sure."

"Do you know what the problem is in this story?" I ask her.

"Ummmm, maybe their cat was sick?"

I take a quick look back at the text. There's a picture of a girl holding a cat and two adults. The cat isn't mentioned in the words of the story.

"Can you tell me more about the cat, Bessie?"

"Well, I'm not really sure, but probably they're going to take it to the vet. We had to do that with my cat last week. Their cat looks just like mine."

I realize with a sinking feeling that Bessie had just "read" this story beautifully, yet understood almost none of it. Although the text is appropriate as measured by her accuracy level, she was unable to comprehend what she read. Bessie needs instruction in comprehension strategies.

A favorite comic strip of mine shows a high school boy trying to complete his entire summer reading book list the day before school starts in the fall. His mother, with an incredulous look on her face, says, "Do you expect me to believe that you read *David Copperfield* walking from the bookstore to the car?" His reply, "Do you want to quibble about comprehension, or do you want me to read books?" is significant. Many students don't connect reading and comprehending. To them, as it was with Bessie, reading is about getting the words right. Comprehension is not an issue. Some of my students even comment, "I read it, but I didn't listen." I think back on my own experience as a parent, when I read bedtime stories to my two sons. I was able to read a familiar story aloud with great fluency and expression, while at the same time making a list in my mind of the jobs I had to do next. Students can also do completely different things in their minds while they are reading and it's difficult to know if they comprehend a text just by listening to them read it. In this chapter we will look at ways to assess comprehension, and how to use the results to plan instruction to help your students get the most out of their reading.

What Is Comprehension?

Comprehension is the reason for reading: to make sense of and understand what is written. The *Report of the National Reading Panel* refers to comprehension as "the essence of reading" (p. 4-39). Without comprehension, there is no true reading. Text comprehension goes beyond a surface-level understanding. It's an active process that involves students' background knowledge, their ongoing understanding of the words and sentences, and the author's intended meaning. True comprehension involves making connections to existing understandings the reader already has to create something new from the text. One reader's understanding of a particular text may differ slightly from another reader's, based on the student's individual background and the connections he or she makes.

To comprehend, students must be able to decode the words accurately. Their phonics skills must be strong enough to read the words. Also, they must be able to understand the vocabulary used in the text. If they don't know the meanings of many individual words, they will not understand the whole. Finally, students must be able to read the text with enough fluency to maintain meaning. Reading too quickly or slowly, or with awkward phrasing, can impede their comprehension.

But it's not enough to read text accurately and with fluency. In order to comprehend, the student has to actively think about and connect with what he or she is reading. Readers use many different strategies that we can teach students to build their comprehension.

What the Research Says About Comprehension

In the past, teachers' editions of classroom reading anthologies came with a list of questions for each story. For comprehension, we asked questions. We acted more like interrogators than teachers. I distinctly remember my helpless feeling when one of my students didn't get the right answer. Now what should I do? There weren't instructions in the anthology for what to do if the student didn't get the right answer. Unfortunately for my students, I often just went on to other students until I found someone who could give me the right answer. Simply asking questions didn't teach comprehension.

In the 1970s, researchers such as David Pearson, Nell Duke, Michael Pressley, and Dolores Durkin examined the behaviors good readers used. They found that good readers:

○ **are active**. They don't simply say words, but search for the meaning by rereading, checking pictures, thinking about what they read, and making connections.

○ **have goals in mind for their reading**. They have a purpose and read in ways to meet their goal.

○ **preview a text and its structure before reading and make predictions as they read**. They don't simply open the book and start reading. Good readers have an idea of what they will be reading about before they start.

○ **integrate prior knowledge with the text**. They use what they know to understand what they read.

○ **monitor their understanding and make adjustments in speed and style as necessary**. They know when they don't comprehend, and take steps to fix the problem.

○ **think about the author**. They identify the author's purpose in writing the text, and how well it was accomplished. They notice things the author did when writing, such as word choice.

○ **react to the text**. They talk about it, make connections, or ask questions.

Educators Ellin Keene and Susan Zimmermann (1997) found that teaching struggling students these "good reader" behaviors improved their ability to comprehend specific text.

Duke and Pearson (2002) maintain that our approach to teaching reading—reflected in our philosophy, our lesson plans, and our classroom environment—can make a difference for our students. Providing students a great deal of time to read real texts for real purposes, and opportunities to read and write the full range of text genres, fosters comprehension. A rich classroom environment that includes talk about text and discussion of words and their meanings and instruction that ensures accuracy in decoding will also have a positive effect on comprehension.

So how do we best teach these strategies? Duke and Pearson suggest that a classroom instructional model with the following five components is effective in teaching comprehension strategies:

● an explicit description of the comprehension strategy and when and how to use it

● modeling of the strategy in action, by teacher and/or students

● collaborative use of the strategy in action

● guided practice with the strategy

● independent use of the strategy

We will take a look at how this instructional model looks in a classroom setting a little later. First, let's see what comprehension strategies we can teach.

COMPREHENSION STRATEGIES

Comprehension strategies are behaviors readers use to understand text. They can be divided into several categories. Before-reading strategies include activities like previewing and making predictions about the text, setting a goal for reading, and accessing background knowledge. During- and after-reading strategies include monitoring understanding, using fix-up strategies, visualizing, questioning, inferring, summarizing, and making connections. I've selected eight strategies that have had the greatest impact on my students. Let's take a look at each, and see how it contributes to comprehension.

Predicting

Predicting is using clues the author and illustrator have provided, along with one's background knowledge, to make good guesses about the text. Students who continually select books from a particular series are predicting that the book will be interesting, based on past experience. Adults often predict the content of a novel based on the author or cover illustration. Good readers predict before they read and continue to make and revise predictions as they read on.

Questioning

Posing and answering questions before, during, and after reading helps readers focus on finding the answers to their questions. Chapters that end with a cliff-hanger are a good example. We read on to find the answer to "What is going to happen next?" Questioning also helps readers make connections, summarize, and make inferences. When my students wondered how the lazy Jamie O'Rourke could grow such a big potato (see page 183), we read the text carefully and examined the illustrations for clues to help them decide on an answer.

Visualizing

Visualizing is making mental images during reading. It can also include making a visual representation of the text in the form of a graphic organizer, diagram, or picture. Visualizing helps readers understand connections and relationships among different parts of the text. For example, when my third-grade students learned from a nonfiction text that the largest wolf ever found weighed 175 pounds, they compared their weights and discovered it would take almost three of them to weigh as much as that one wolf. They also sketched wolves based on the descriptions in the text to better understand how wolves are camouflaged in the forest.

Connecting

Connecting is when a reader links something from a reading to his or her life, another book, or something in the world. For example, when I read *Blueberries for Sal*, one of my students remarked that it reminded her of picking blackberries with her family. Later, when we read *Blackberries* in guided reading group, she made a connection between Baby Bear eating all of his blackberries and Sal eating almost all her blueberries. Another student connected Baby Bear getting lost to a news report of a scout getting lost during a camping trip. As they make these meaningful connections, readers better understand what they read.

Monitoring

Engaged readers monitor themselves, checking to see if what they are reading is making sense. They notice when they do not understand, and take steps to repair this breakdown in comprehension. Monitoring habits include stopping and rereading, checking pictures, slowing the pace, or trying to clarify word or sentence meanings. If we aren't monitoring, the chances of our comprehending a text are low. Students who substitute words that may visually resemble the correct word but don't make sense are often not monitoring their comprehension. For example, one student read, "The newborn pups are now members of the wolf park." He stopped and correctly reread the text as, "The newborn pups are now members of the wolf pack," showing that he successfully monitored his understanding.

Summarizing

Summarizing is synthesizing and determining the important ideas in a text. It requires the ability to see the big picture and the main idea. It helps readers to determine the author's purpose and message or theme. For many students, this is particularly difficult. Students may be able to tell all the events that occurred in a story such as "Goldilocks and the Three Bears," but pick up very little of the author's message beyond the very literal idea that "you should lock your door when you go out," as one student suggested.

Inferring

Inferring refers to drawing conclusions based on evidence in a text along with one's background knowledge. It is often referred to as "reading between the lines," making assumptions about reasons for things that happen in a text, as well as figuring out what might happen as a result of action in a text. Unlike predictions, inferences cannot always be confirmed or discounted as you read on. Much of what we decide about characters is based on inferences about their actions, what they say, and what others say about them. Many words require readers to make inferences based on the context of the sentences.

Younger students often struggle with inferences, since they tend to think quite literally. When faced with an inferential question, my students sometimes respond, "But it doesn't say!" I have to teach them to look for the clues the author has provided. For example, when discussing "Goldilocks and the Three Bears," we might discuss how Papa Bear knew that someone had been sitting in his chair. What clues did Goldilocks leave? Perhaps she left a dent in the cushions. Maybe she moved the chair a little bit, or moved something that was on it. Asking questions such as "Would Goldilocks be a good friend?" encourages students to look at her behavior for clues about her character, such as the fact that she helped herself to food, and broke things, but didn't seem very sorry.

Using Text Structure

Using text structure is considering the important elements and organization of a text as a framework for understanding and recalling important ideas. Elements of fiction include setting, characters, events, a problem, and a resolution, as well as an overarching theme. Nonfiction also has various

Patterns of Text Structures in Informational Text

Text pattern	Definition	Key words	Graphic organizer
Description	Helps reader form images or visualize processes	For example, on, over, beyond, and descriptive adjectives	Web
Sequence	Presents ideas or events in the order that they happen	First, second, before, next, then, finally, later, last	Flow chart
Compare and contrast	Discusses two ideas, showing how they are similar and different	While, but, yet, rather, most, on the other hand	Venn diagram
Cause and effect	Provides explanations and reasons for events	Because, since so that, if then	Flow chart
Problem and solution	Identifies problems and poses solutions	The problem, propose, a reason for	Web or flow chart

organizational structures. Using these structures and elements helps readers remember and pick out the main ideas of a text. For example, my students generally gain a better understanding of a text about frogs and toads if they recognize that it is written to compare and contrast, rather than to provide information in sequential order. I use visuals like those in the chart on page 157, to distinguish these differences.

These eight strategies all contribute to comprehension, and we often use several of them at once. Because reading is a mental process, it's often difficult to assess whether or not students are using these strategies. Students show us evidence of the strategies that they use by demonstrating an understanding of a specific text.

We start with checking for overall comprehension—can students tell us in general about what they've read? Then we move to whether and how effectively students are using comprehension strategies.

General Comprehension Assessments

Here are several specific assessments that will give you information about how effectively students are comprehending text.

ANALYZING ERRORS

We can get an initial idea about students' comprehension by listening to them read aloud and analyzing the kinds of errors they make, as we saw in Chapter 1. Errors that show an overreliance on visual cues at the expense of meaning send up a red flag. Errors that make sense, like substituting *might* for *may*, indicate that the reader is reading for meaning and understanding at least to some degree. Yet, sometimes students make no errors as they read aloud, even when they do not understand. As my experience with Bessie showed, we can't assume students fully comprehend what they are reading. How else can we assess comprehension?

INFORMAL READING INVENTORY

The Informal Reading Inventories (IRIs) we discussed in Chapter 1 come with a set of questions for each text to assess students' understanding. IRI questions are usually divided into several categories, including *literal*, *inferential*, and *evaluative* questions. Students' answers to these questions show how they are thinking as they read and how well they are understanding the text. However, the quality of the information we get from these questions is not always as good as we would hope.

A sample IRI passage and accompanying questions for a fifth-grade text appear below. It includes too few questions to give us an adequate picture of students' comprehension, most questions are too text-based, and many can be answered with students' prior knowledge. This example includes only two literal "fact" questions (labeled F), two based on making an inference (I), and one on vocabulary (V). Both fact questions require students to recall only minor details from the very end of the text. The inferential questions do not require students to use information from the text to answer, and the assessed word, *coast*, is in most fifth-grade students' vocabulary already.

FORM A: Pretest   **Part 2/Level 5 (167 Words)**

Background Knowledge Assessment: What do you know about pirates?

Adequate [ ]   Inadequate [ ]

PIRATES!

Comprehension Check

Pirates were people who attacked and robbed ships. They raided towns like Charleston, South Carolina. Most people who became pirates hoped to get rich. Most pirates were men. A few women became pirates, too.

Movies have given us the idea that pirates led exciting lives. In real life, however, most pirates led miserable lives. Many pirates died of wounds or disease. Many were captured and hanged.

In the early 1700s, South Carolina was a colony. Pirates sailed along the coast. They robbed ships sailing to or from Charleston. There were so many pirates around Charleston that few ships were safe.

One of these pirates was Stede Bonnet. Bonnet sailed with another pirate named Blackbeard. Bonnet was very mean. He was the first pirate to make people "walk the plank."

William Rhett set out to capture Bonnet. He did, and took Bonnet and his crew to Charleston. All of Bonnet's crew were hanged. Just before Bonnet was to be hanged, a friend took him some women's clothes. Dressed as a woman, Bonnet was able to escape. Rhett went after him again. Bonnet was brought back to Charleston and hanged.

Pirates are gone now, but their stories live on.

(F) 1. _____ How did Bonnet escape from jail? (He dressed as a woman)

(F) 2. _____ What happened to Bonnet? (He was hanged)

(I) 3. _____ Why do you think some women become pirates? (Any reasonable answer; e.g., they wanted to get rich; they were married to pirates; they thought it would be exciting)

(V) 4. _____ What does the word "coast" mean in this story? (Where the land meets the sea; the beach)

(I) 5. _____ What do you think "walk the plank" means? (The pirates forced people to walk on a board until they fell overboard)

Scoring Guide   Fifth

SIG WR Errors		COMP Errors	
IND	2	IND	0–1
INST	8	INST	1½–2
FRUST	17+	FRUST	2½+

Inventory Record for Teachers, FORM A: Pretest   61

Sample IRI test, grade 5

Unfortunately, this example is typical. Mary DeKonty Applegate and her colleagues (2002) found that more than 90 percent of the items on eight popular commercial IRIs either assessed literal knowledge or the ability to make an inference so close to literal as to be obvious. The questions were overwhelmingly text-based, involving the lowest levels of thinking. An IRI like this wouldn't provide us with much information beyond students' ability to simply recall a text. In addition, when questions can be answered simply by relying on background knowledge, we can't know if the student comprehended the text, or simply knew the answer already. Recently when I was assessing a fourth-grade student using an IRI passage about beavers, one of the questions asked what a beaver's tail looked like. Although the student had been unable to read most of the passage with accuracy, she knew what a beaver looked like since it is the mascot of one of our local universities. She answered that one question correctly, although it was apparent from her responses to the other questions that she hadn't comprehended much of what she read.

If you are asked to use an IRI and the accompanying questions, look very closely at the items. You may need to rewrite or add questions in order to get a true picture of students' abilities, or you may choose to use another way to assess comprehension, such as retelling.

RETELLINGS

Rather than use the complete IRI tool, I prefer to have students read the passage provided and retell what they've read. This way, students have to consider the whole text rather than just respond to a few questions. Retelling involves summarizing, organizing, and synthesizing information from the text, not simply recalling literal information to answer a question. However, retellings are still not the perfect assessment tool, since they are a contrived task. We don't usually read a text and then tell everything we remember. Some students may not understand the task. Some are naturally shy and become uncomfortable if retellings have not been part of their instruction. Therefore, it is important that you have modeled retellings before using them as an assessment.

An oral retelling is conducted between teacher and student. It can be a follow-up to a running record or informal reading inventory, or you can ask students to retell something they've just read silently in a guided reading group or during independent reading. Steps for a formal assessment follow.

Procedure

1. Select a text for the student to read. The text should be at his or her instructional reading level (see Chapter 1 for a discussion of this). You can select either narrative or expository text. Narrative text is generally easier to retell if it has a clear plot.

2. Let the student know that you will be asking him or her to retell after reading.

3. Ask the student to read the text silently (or orally if you're doing an accuracy assessment as well).

4. After the student has finished, ask him or her to put the text aside and retell everything he or she can remember.

5. Record the student's responses on a copy of a recording form for narrative or nonfiction retellings (pages 163 and 164).

6. Use prompts or follow-up questions as necessary. (Page 162 provides a list of prompts.)

7. Analyze and score the retelling for completeness. Indicate the quality of each response with a number from 1 to 5, with 1 being the least amount of detail and information, and 5 being the most complete description of the item. Mark whether each item is included in the initial retelling or if you prompted the student with a general prompt, a direct question, or encouraged him or her to reread the text to locate the information.

You may decide to let students look back in the text to locate particular items. I often allow my students to do this, depending on the length and complexity of the text. It can be overwhelming to try to remember many events or details after just one reading. If my students still can't locate an important element of the retelling, such as Baby Bear finding his chair broken, I know that their comprehension on this particular text is questionable.

To facilitate your record keeping, you may select key events in a narrative text ahead of time, and check off which of the items the students are able to retell, with or without prompting. This is especially helpful if you will be using the same text with many children. You might create a form similar to that on page 165, a retelling record form for "Goldilocks and the Three Bears." In this case, you can simply check off the events as the student tells them, and make comments as to whether they were in sequence or not. You can still judge the quality of the description of the setting and characters using a numeric score.

Retelling Prompts for Fiction and Nonfiction

General prompts for fiction retellings include:

● What was this story about?

● Can you tell me any more about that?

● Can you remember anything else?

Direct questions include:

● Who was the main character and what was he or she like?

● When and where did the story take place?

● Who else was in the story?

● What was the problem?

● What happened after that?

● How did they solve the problem?

● What did this remind you of?

● What was the main idea of this story?

● Was there a part of the story that surprised you?

● What do you think might happen next time?

Your prompting questions will be different for expository text. Direct questions for nonfiction retellings include:

● What was the text mostly about?

● What was the author's main message?

● How did the author support the main idea?

● What did you learn?

● What do you think the author wanted you to learn?

● How did the author organize the text?

Similarly, if you will be using a particular nonfiction text to assess many students, you might want to record important information on a form like the one on page 166, so you can easily check each item off as the student retells.

Obviously, if students have not had instruction about these elements of nonfiction, you would not expect them to be able to discuss text organization and author's purpose. You will tailor the recording form and prompts to fit the specific text and what you want to find out about students' comprehension.

RECORDING FORM FOR RETELLING OF A NARRATIVE TEXT

Name _____ Date _____

Text _____ Level _____

	Initial retelling	Prompt	Question	With rereading
1. Setting	____	____	____	____
Comments:				
2. Character and description				
main character	____	____	____	____
other characters	____	____	____	____
Comments:				
3. Plot events				
problem or goal	____	____	____	____
important events in order	____	____	____	____
resolution or ending	____	____	____	____
Comments:				
4. Main idea	____	____	____	____
Comments:				
5. Inferences or conclusions based on evidence	____	____	____	____
Comments:				

Key

1: minimal information   **3:** adequate   **5:** very complete information

RECORDING FORM FOR RETELLING OF A NONFICTION TEXT

Name _____ Date _____

Text _____ Level _____

	Initial retelling	Prompt	Question	With rereading
1. **Identifies topic**	_____	_____	_____	_____
Comments:				
2. **Identifies main idea**	_____	_____	_____	_____
Comments:				
3. **Recalls important details**	_____	_____	_____	_____
Comments:				
4. **Identifies text structure**	_____	_____	_____	_____
Comments:				
5. **Identifies author's purpose**	_____	_____	_____	_____
Comments:				

Key

1: minimal information   **3:** adequate   **5:** very complete information

Name _____ Date _____

Text _____Goldilocks and the Three Bears_____ Level _____

	Initial retelling	Prompt	Question	With rereading
1. Setting				
Long ago in the forest in the Three Bears' house	_____	_____	_____	_____
2. Characters				
Goldilocks	_____	_____	_____	_____
Papa Bear	_____	_____	_____	_____
Mama Bear	_____	_____	_____	_____
Baby Bear	_____	_____	_____	_____
3. Plot events				
Mama Bear makes porridge	_____	_____	_____	_____
They go for a walk to let it cool	_____	_____	_____	_____
Goldilocks comes in	_____	_____	_____	_____
She tries all three chairs	_____	_____	_____	_____
She breaks Baby Bear's chair	_____	_____	_____	_____
She tries all three porridges	_____	_____	_____	_____
She eats all of Baby Bear's	_____	_____	_____	_____
She tries all three beds	_____	_____	_____	_____
She falls asleep in Baby Bear's	_____	_____	_____	_____
The bears come home	_____	_____	_____	_____
They find the broken chair	_____	_____	_____	_____
They find the eaten porridge	_____	_____	_____	_____
They find Goldilocks	_____	_____	_____	_____
She runs away	_____	_____	_____	_____
4. Main idea	_____	_____	_____	_____
5. Inferences or conclusion	_____	_____	_____	_____

Comments:

Key

1: minimal information   **3:** adequate   **5:** very complete information

RECORDING FORM FOR RETELLING OF *ANIMAL HOMES*

Name _____ Date _____

Text ___Animal Homes_____ Level ___12___

	Initial retelling	Prompt	Question	With rereading
1. Identifies topic animal homes	____	____	____	____
2. Identifies main idea animal homes are different	____	____	____	____
3. Recalls important details	____	____	____	____
• some animals (squirrels) build homes in trees	____	____	____	____
• some animals (rabbits) dig holes underground	____	____	____	____
• some animals (beavers) make homes in water	____	____	____	____
• some animals (bats) make their homes in caves	____	____	____	____
4. Identifies text structure description, compare/contrast	____	____	____	____
5. Identifies author's purpose teach/inform about animal homes	____	____	____	____

Key

1: minimal information   **3:** adequate   **5:** very complete information

Written Retelling Alternative

In some cases, you may decide to ask students to do a written retelling of a text. This may include drawing, writing, or completing a graphic organizer appropriate to the text. A retelling frame like the one on page 168 can be helpful for students. Use sentence starters that are appropriate for the text they will be reading.

Written retellings can be especially valuable with older or more capable students, but they may not give a true picture of reading comprehension, since the information gathered is filtered through students' ability to communicate in writing. Therefore, following a written retelling, plan to meet with students individually and use specific prompts or questions to elicit further responses as necessary.

ANALYZING RETELLINGS

The next step is taking a look at student responses. A record of a retelling done by a second-grade student, Jake, appears below. Jake was able to understand the main idea and make inferences about the whole text. He had difficulties with remembering individual events and identifying the problem and resolution of the story. After prompting and questioning, he was able to identify them.

Name _Jake_   Date _4/26_
Text _Fred Goes Shopping_   Level _2.1_

	Initial Retelling	Prompt	Question	With Rereading
1. Setting	5	___	___	___
2. Character and Description				
main character	4			
other characters	2/4	✓	___	___
3. Plot Events				
problem or goal	2/4	✓	✓	___
important events in order	3			
resolution or ending	2/4	✓	✓	___
4. Main Idea	4	___	___	___
5. Inferences or Conclusions based on evidence	4	___	___	___

Key
1: minimal information   3: adequate   5: very complete information

Comments:
Got the big idea.
Had trouble remembering beginning
events. Distracted by pictures.
Didn't realize until prompted that
Fred got extras.

Second-grader Jake's retelling assessment

Story Retelling Frame

Name _____ Date _____

Title _____

Author _____

This story takes place _____

_____

The main character is _____

who _____

Some other characters are _____

A problem happens when _____

_____

After that _____

_____

_____

The problem is solved when _____

_____

At the end of the story _____

_____

The main idea of this story is _____

_____

The author wanted me to _____

_____

Jake would benefit from practice with strategies for using text structure to organize story events, and asking and answering questions to identify problems and solutions in the text. While he appears to be reading actively, I would next give him an assessment using nonfiction, to see if he can support main ideas with details.

Strategy Use Assessments

Retellings let you know if a student understands a specific text, but they don't tell you which comprehension strategies he or she used along the way. If you find gaps in comprehension, you will want to assess the strategies the student is using. Even without gaps, knowing which strategies students use is helpful for planning classroom comprehension instruction. For example, do students make connections while reading? Do they predict before reading, or ask questions to help them focus? Which of the eight strategies described earlier in the chapter are students successfully using across a broad range of text?

There are several ways to get this kind of information, the first of which is a self-assessment. How Did I Do Today? (page 170) is one assessment students can use after reading a fiction text to indicate what they did before, during, and after reading. The nonfiction version appears on page 171. These two forms are appropriate to use with students at or above the third-grade level who have been taught the full range of comprehension strategies. Adjust the content for the level of students you work with and the strategies you have taught. For example, you may choose to include only items concerning predicting and visualizing, if those are two strategies you expect students to use. You may simplify the language to tailor it for students in first and second grades. Whatever you decide to include in the self-assessment will determine what you can find out about your students' strategy use.

There is a danger in relying too heavily on self-assessments for your data. Students may simply mark what they know are good strategies, whether they've actually used them or not. In order to really see if students are using these strategies, observe them carefully during guided reading lessons and discuss their reading in conferences during independent reading time.

> ### Resources for Retelling Assessment
>
> There are a number of commercial programs available that include leveled texts along with retelling recording forms for the texts. These materials ensure that students have not read the assessment text before, and some of the forms offer specific prompts, key points from the text, and a way to organize your findings.
>
> *Developmental Reading Assessment (2nd ed.)* by J. Beaver & M. Carter (Celebration Press)
>
> *Fountas & Pinnell Benchmark Assessment System* by I. C. Fountas & G. Pinnell (Heinemann)
>
> *On-the-Mark Assessment* (Wright Group/McGraw Hill)
>
> *Rigby PM Ultra Benchmark Kit* (Harcourt Achieve)

How Did I Do Today? (Fiction Reading)

Text _____ Date _____

Strategies I Used Before I Read Today

_____ I thought about the cover and title.

_____ I asked questions in my head. Here is one I thought of:

_____ I predicted what I might learn. Here is a prediction I made:

Strategies I Used While I Was Reading

_____ I stopped to see if I understood what I was reading.

_____ I made pictures in my head as I read.

_____ I found the confusing parts and unknown words.

_____ I reread to understand confusing parts and words.

_____ I predicted and adjusted my predictions as I read.

_____ I wondered and read for answers.

_____ I made connections to myself, other texts, and the world.

Strategies I Used After I Read

_____ I thought about the author's message.

_____ I reread to find details.

_____ I thought about the characters, setting, and plot events.

How Did I Do Today? (Nonfiction Reading)

Text _____ Date _____

Strategies I Used Before I Read Today

_____ I looked at the cover and title to determine the topic.

_____ I thought about what I already know about the topic.

_____ I asked questions in my head. Here is one I thought of:

_____ I looked at the pictures, charts, and graphs.

_____ I read the headings and words in bold.

_____ I predicted what I might learn. Here is a prediction I made:

Strategies I Used While I Was Reading

_____ I stopped to see if I understood what I was reading.

_____ I made mental pictures.

_____ I identified confusing parts and unknown words.

_____ I reread to understand confusing parts and words.

_____ I used pictures, graphs, and charts to help me understand.

_____ I stopped and retold to check what I remember.

_____ I read the captions under and above photographs.

_____ I predicted and adjusted my predictions as I read.

_____ I raised questions and read for answers.

Strategies I Used After I Read

_____ I thought about what I learned. Here is one thing:

_____ I connected my new learning with what I already knew about the topic.

_____ I reread to find details.

_____ I shared what I learned with someone else.

Many of the activities that follow for teaching the strategies can also serve as good informal assessments as you observe how students complete the tasks. For example, Roll and Ask, an activity used to develop questioning skills, is also useful for assessing students' abilities to select important details from the text, and answer questions posed by their peers. Students who continually pick out unimportant details, such as asking what color Baby Bear's chair was, indicate they don't understand what's worth remembering in the text.

PLAN

Once you've assessed your students' comprehension and what strategies they seem to be using, it's time to design instruction. You will do some whole-group instruction to introduce, model, and practice comprehension strategies that students have not yet mastered. You will also provide opportunities for students to practice strategies on appropriate leveled texts in small-group situations, such as guided reading groups. In some cases, you will design instruction for intervention groups of students who are still struggling.

Strategy Use Recording Form (Third-Grade Example)

Strategies observed with: • (fiction) • expository • poetry (circle appropriate genre) Shared (S) Guided (G) Independent (I)	Makes predictions	Asks and answers questions	Monitors and uses fix-up strategies	Visualizes	Uses text structure	Summarizes	Infers	Makes connections
	S G I	S G I	S G I	S G I	S G I	S G I	S G I	S G I
George	✓ ✓ ✓	✓ ✓	✓	✓	✓		✓	✓

STRATEGY USE RECORDING FORM

Strategies observed with: • fiction • expository • poetry (circle appropriate genre) **Shared (S)** **Guided (G)** **Independent (I)**	Makes predictions	Asks and answers questions	Monitors and uses fix-up strategies	Visualizes	Uses text structure	Summarizes	Infers	Makes connections
	S G I	S G I	S G I	S G I	S G I	S G I	S G I	S G I

In order to do this planning, it is helpful to use a strategy recording sheet, similar to the matrix used in Chapter 1. The form shown on page 173 has all eight of the strategies included, but you may want to include only those strategies that you have modeled and expect students to use at a particular time of the year.

Keep track of the situations in which students are exhibiting a particular strategy, such as during, shared, guided, and independent reading, as shown in the example on page 172. Often students are able to use the strategies when you are guiding them, but cannot do so independently. Ultimately, we will know that students have mastered the strategies when they use them in independent reading. You may want to include a date for when the strategies were used. Also keep track of the genres to which students have success-fully applied the strategies. I keep separate class records for three kinds of text: fiction, expository text, and poetry.

The chart below will help you design instruction and activities to support the use of comprehension strategies. As you assess students' comprehen-sion, you may find that they do not exhibit many of the behaviors of good readers discussed at the beginning of this chapter. For example, they may not be active readers, who search for meaning by rereading, checking pictures, thinking about what they read, and making connections. Notice that many of the activities are listed more than once, since they support several behaviors and comprehension strategies.

If the student . . .	You might teach these comprehension strategies . . .	Using these activities in the classroom . . .	Page number
is not active when reading	predicting visualizing questioning inferring using text structure summarizing connecting monitoring	• KWL Charts	178
		• Prediction Papers	181
		• I Wonder	181
		• Sketch It	183
		• Where Did That Come From?	184
		• Read a Handful and Retell	185
		• Mark It	186
		• Roll and Ask	186
		• Question-Answer Relationships (QAR)	187
		• Stop and Talk/Write	197
		• Reciprocal Teaching	197

If the student . . .	You might teach these comprehension strategies . . .	Using these activities in the classroom . . .	Page number
does not preview and make predictions when reading	predicting questioning connecting using text structure	● Picture Walk Book Introduction ● Text Features Stroll ● Important Words ● Prediction Papers ● I Wonder ● Stop and Talk/Write ● Reciprocal Teaching	178 178 179 181 181 197 197
does not set goals for reading	predicting questioning visualizing using text structure monitoring connecting	● I Wonder ● Sketch It ● Roll and Ask ● Graphic Organizers ● Retelling Cards for Fiction ● Reciprocal Teaching	181 183 186 188 194 197
does not monitor reading	visualizing questioning summarizing monitoring	● Read a Handful and Retell ● Mark It ● Reciprocal Teaching	185 186 197
has difficulty retelling story events or details in expository text	summarizing visualizing text structure questioning monitoring	● Sketch It ● Question-Answer Relationships ● Graphic Organizers ● Story Star ● Retelling Cards for Fiction ● Somewhere, Sometime, Somebody Retell ● Draw and Tell ● Stop and Talk/Write ● Reciprocal Teaching	183 187 188 188 194 197 197 197 197
does not summarize or identify main ideas	visualizing connecting inferring monitoring	● Sketch It ● Graphic Organizers ● Story Star ● Stop and Talk/Write ● Reciprocal Teaching	183 188 188 197 197
does not integrate prior knowledge and make inferences	visualizing connecting inferring questioning	● I Wonder ● Sketch It ● Where Did That Come From? ● Roll and Ask ● Question-Answer Relationships ● Reciprocal Teaching ● Language Experience	181 183 184 186 187 197 200

TEACH

Teaching Model for New Strategies

● Description of the strategy

● Modeling

● Collaborative use

● Guided practice

● Independent use

When teaching comprehension strategies, it is important to remember Duke and Pearson's teaching model at the beginning of this chapter (page 154, summarized at left). The sequence of instruction begins with "a clear description of the strategy and why and when to use it." For example, you might say to your students, "Today I am going to share with you a strategy that helps you understand what you read, called *predicting*. Predicting means making good guesses about what might be in the text you are reading. It helps you make sense of what you read and to be active and involved, rather than just letting words wash over you. Predicting keeps your mind focused as you read to see if you are right in your prediction. You should make predictions before you begin reading a text, and continue as you read."

Next comes modeling of the strategy in action. I find it works best to do this as part of a teacher read-aloud or shared reading. This way, all of the students have access to the text without regard to their decoding abilities, and they can focus on what you are doing as you read and share your thinking.

You might say something like this: "I am going to show you what I'm thinking about as I read this book and make predictions. First, I will look at the cover. I see a rhinoceros and a very strange-looking animal that might be a porcupine. They look like they are friends. Then I look at the title, *A Porcupine Named Fluffy*. So it is a porcupine. I predict he will be the main character. But I think there's going to be a problem. Porcupines aren't supposed to be fluffy. Perhaps the rhino will help him solve his problem. I see the author is Helen Lester. I've read some other books she's written, and they are usually really funny. The main character often learns a good lesson, too. So I think the porcupine will learn a lesson about being fluffy. Now I will open the book and start reading. The predictions I've made are helping me pay attention to what I'm reading to see if I'm correct." As I read the story to my students, I stop often to check out my prediction and ask students to help me tell whether it was confirmed or not. I make other predictions, and read on to see if I am correct.

The next step is collaborative use of the strategy in action. During my initial read-aloud, after I've done some modeling, I often ask students to try out the strategy and share their thinking, like this: "I've made some good predictions that are helping me understand this story. Now I'd like you to help make some predictions. Stop right now and think about what might happen next. . . . Let's hear what predictions you've made, and why."

Next in the teaching sequence is guided practice. I usually do this in the context of a guided reading lesson. Make sure the text you are using for developing new comprehension strategies is well within the students' instructional reading level. I often use text that could be considered independent level, where they know at least 95 percent of the words, because I do not want students to be hung up on decoding of words. I want them to be able to focus their thinking on making sense and applying the new strategy.

In this and the next stage, the activities that I have included in the following section can be used to assist students in using specific comprehension strategies. For example, if you are using the Important Words activity on page 179 to build prediction skills, you might share six or seven words you've selected from the text the students will be reading and say something like this, "These are some words I've taken from the book you will be reading today. They will help you make some predictions about the text. Let's take a look at the words. They are *castle, knights, gates, spit, hero, digging*. Think about these words and how they may fit into the story. Let's hear your ideas. . . . Now, as we read today, I will ask you to check to see if your predictions are coming true. Every few pages I will ask you to stop and make a new prediction. Pay attention to how making these predictions is helping you make sense as you read."

Finally, students are ready for independent use of the strategy. Say, "As you read today, remember about making predictions. Be sure to make predictions every few pages. Ask yourself why you are making each prediction—what are your clues? Check to see if your predictions come true. Notice how this helps you read."

The rest of this chapter includes suggestions for instructional activities that encourage the use of the comprehension strategies. As you can see from the planning chart on pages 174 and 175, the activities may encourage the use of several of the strategies. For example, when you pose questions before reading, you are using questioning but you naturally begin to predict the answer. A strategy like I Wonder (page 181) will encourage the use of both questioning and predicting. *The Report of the National Reading Panel* (p. 4-46) recommends using strategies in conjunction with one another in this way, as opposed to using them in isolation. Let's take a look at the activities.

Before-Reading Activities

PICTURE WALK BOOK INTRODUCTION
(Large or small group, individual)

Your youngest readers rely on pictures to communicate information about the text. "Walking" students through the text and discussing the pictures is an effective method for helping them develop some predictions. I find it most helpful to let the students do most of the talking, so that they are the ones making the predictions. I often pose questions such as "Why do you suppose Mother Bear is looking at her watch?" to encourage some inferences as well. A Picture Walk is also the perfect time to introduce unusual language patterns or difficult vocabulary words like this: "The balloon in this story is very rude. He keeps telling everyone to 'jump in a sack.' It's kind of like telling someone to go jump in a lake. Have you ever said that?"

TEXT FEATURES STROLL (Large or small group, individual)

As your students read expository text, the Picture Walk changes into a Text Features Stroll. In this activity, lead students through the text, stopping to notice and discuss the table of contents, headings, introduction, visuals such as graphs, charts, and illustrations, and highlighted vocabulary words. Ask students to use the text features to make predictions about the text structure and what they will be reading about. Our goal is for students to ultimately be able to skim a text and use the text features to predict on their own.

KWL CHARTS (Large or small group, individual)

KWL (What We KNOW, What We WANT to Learn, What We LEARNED) charts are tried-and-true activities to help students predict as well as ask questions and access background knowledge before they read. I have had success using KWL charts with both fiction and expository text.

● Draw a KWL chart, consisting of three columns, as shown on page 179. You can make copies of the chart on page 180 for students.

Explain to the class (or remind them) that the first column shows what we already think we know about a topic.

● Have students, either collectively or individually, on their own charts, complete a list in this column. I find it very helpful to continually ask students, "How do you know that?" as they give me items for this first section. In a group situation, these questions help other students see how they can access different kinds of background knowledge to help them understand a text.

● Guide students to respond to the next section, which includes what we want to learn about the topic. This is where students pose questions and make predictions based on our Picture Walk or Text Features Stroll. Finally, after reading, we record what we learned from the text. Below is a KWL chart developed for *The Toll Bridge Troll* by Patricia Rae Wolf.

KWL Chart for *The Toll Bridge Troll*

What we know about trolls	What we want to find out about this troll	What we learned about trolls
They live under bridges. They are mean. They eat goats. They are in *Harry Potter*. Some of them are cute and live in Iceland.	Why does he have on that hat? What's a toll bridge? Will he eat that boy? Is he mean? Does he live under the bridge?	They aren't very smart. They don't usually go to school. They think mothers are important. They are greedy. He doesn't eat the boy. He wants to collect money to cross the bridge. I think he lives under the bridge.

IMPORTANT WORDS (Large or small group, individual)

In addition to providing comprehension practice, Important Words is also a good way to informally assess prior knowledge and vocabulary and do some instruction if you discover students do not have enough prior knowledge to comprehend a text. Ask individual students to define the words and use them in sentences, or share the connections that they've made regarding the words.

● Select six or seven important words or phrases from the text. For fiction, you might select words describing the setting, the main characters, or the problem. For example, if students were going to read a version of "Goldilocks," you might include *porridge, broken, asleep, naughty, cottage,*

KWL Chart

What we know about _____	What we want to find out about _____	What we learned about _____

little girl. For expository text, select words from different categories students will learn about. For example, for a description of lions, you might choose *streamlined, mane, pride, predator, African plains, attack, sharp teeth, claws.*

● Either write the words on the chalkboard or provide students with the words on individual cards. Students can use them to make predictions, identify possible characters, problems, or settings, or sort words into categories, such as physical description and habitat.

● After reading, students can also use the important words as prompts to summarize or retell the text.

Variation: Instead of providing students with the words, ask students to predict important words they expect to find in the text after a Picture Walk or Text Features Stroll. Make a list of these words and after reading see how many words were in the text. If a word was not in the text, discuss why it may not have been included.

PREDICTION PAPERS (Large or small group, individual)

The short form Predicting What a Text Is About (page 182) is a useful tool for encouraging students to make predictions before they read a text. Predictions can be based on Important Words, pictures, the title, or items they've noticed during a Text Features Stroll, such as the table of contents. Students make their predictions before reading, and afterward tell whether their prediction was accurate, along with an explanation of what was in the text.

I WONDER (Large or small group, individual)

In I Wonder, students pose questions before, during, and after reading a text. For my initial instruction, I like to record the students' questions on a large chart, separated into three sections: before, during, and after. In a group situation, I may write students' names next to their questions. As I read, I stop often to see if any questions have been answered. If so, we check them off as answered. Questions which remain unanswered from direct reading of the text require us to do some inferential or evaluative reasoning to decide the answers. Occasionally, we don't find the answers at all. A chart of questions posed for *Jamie O'Rourke and the Big Potato* by Tomie de Paola (Putnam, 1997) appears on page 183. Notice some of our last questions, which required drawing inferences, are not checked off.

Predicting What a Text Is About

Name _____ Date _____

Based on _____

I think this text will be about _____
_____

I think this because _____
_____
_____

My prediction was confirmed/not confirmed because _____
_____
_____

✂ ···

Name _____ Date _____

Based on _____

I think this text will be about _____
_____

I think this because _____
_____
_____

My prediction was confirmed/not confirmed because _____
_____
_____

As students become more familiar with this strategy, they write their own questions in writing journals or on sticky notes in their text, and record their answers. In a guided reading group, students may place their sticky notes on the answer to questions if they locate them while reading independently.

Questions Generated About a Text Before, During, and After Reading

Our Questions About *Jamie O'Rourke and the Big Potato*

Before reading

> How did he get that big potato? ✓
> Did he grow it? ✓
> Did the leprechaun help him? ✓
> What will he do with the potato? ✓

During reading

> What's a "pratie"? ✓
> How does he grow a big potato if he's so lazy? ✓
> Is that the leprechaun making that noise? ✓
> How will they get that potato out of there? ✓
> How can they eat it all? ✓

After reading

> Will Jamie ever find that leprechaun again?
> Does the leprechaun think he was smarter than Jamie? ✓
> Did he really have no money, or did he lie?

During-Reading and After-Reading Activities

SKETCH IT (Large or small group, individual)

This activity can be done during a teacher read-aloud, a guided reading lesson, or individual reading. Students need only paper and pencil. After a section of text is read, ask students to pause and sketch the visual images they have in their heads. Then ask them to share with a partner or the whole group, explaining what clues in the text gave them these images.

Variation: Students sketch their image, and then locate and highlight or write down the words or phrases from the text that contributed to their image.

WHERE DID THAT COME FROM?
(Large or small group, individual)

This activity is similar to Sketch It, but it involves thinking about the way the illustrator conveyed the meaning of the text. Many of the books my students read have pictures. I ask students to use highlighting tape or sticky notes to locate the sentence (or part) in the text that matches what is shown in the picture. Just what part of the text is the illustrator showing in the picture? This requires students to think hard about what is shown in the illustration, and consider the sequence of events and details discussed in the text.

The text shown below, from *What a Day* by Sally Ferrell Odgers (1987), is a good example. At first glance, one might think that the last sentence about the creature next door should be highlighted. But if you examine the picture and think about the text, it's clear that the dog hasn't noticed the creature yet. This always leads to a good discussion about why the cat is shown in the drawing. He's been watching all the time, but right now, the dog doesn't see him. The dog is getting his tail caught in the door.

It started this morning when the old rooster down the road crowed. Well, any dog who calls himself a dog would have to take up a challenge like that, wouldn't he? I made a dive for the dogflap in the kitchen door. I was just launching into my most deepthroated, threatening *woo-woo-woof*, guaranteed to scare the tail feathers off any rooster, when somehow I got my tail caught in the flap as it swung shut. My *woo-woo-woof* turned into an *ow-wow-wow*.

That sort of thing makes a dog feel rather silly. I was licking my poor tail when I heard a snigger. I looked up and – wouldn't you know it? That creature from next door was perched on the garden fence, with its tail in a half hoop and its whiskers folded back. It smirked, "Nice morning."

3

Circling or highlighting the exact part of the text to which the illustration refers calls for close attention to details on this page from *What a Day*.

Sometimes students need to mark parts of more than one sentence. And sometimes, the illustration is based on an inference the illustrator made, depicting an event or information that isn't shown in actual text, but clearly makes sense and must have happened. I love it when this happens because it leads to a great discussion of the reader's responsibility to make sense while reading. The author expects that you will be thinking and understanding that certain events must have happened.

For younger students who are reading books with only a few sentences on each page, cover the text and picture with a sheet of plastic film, such as an overhead transparency or the leftover edges from a laminating project. Ask students to circle words in the text and draw a line to the part of the picture that matches it, as shown below on the pages of *The Fox who Foxed* by Beverly Randell (1996) .

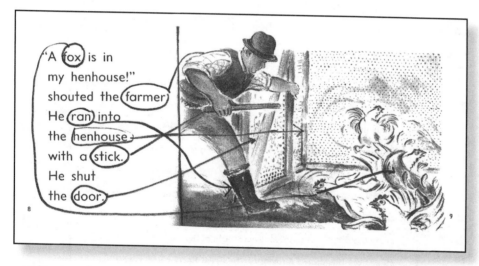

Making simple connections between the text and pictures helps primary readers make meaning and reinforces vocabulary.

READ A HANDFUL AND RETELL
(Large or small group, individual)

As students are reading, I ask them to read about as much text as their hands can cover (a handful). Then I ask them to stop and retell the information or events to themselves to check to see if it makes sense. If they do not feel confident that they have understood the text, they reread. You can also have students work with partners to read a handful, stop, think about what they've read, and retell it to their partners. This activity encourages students to monitor themselves.

MARK IT (Large or small group, individual)

This is especially valuable for reading nonfiction text. Give students a copy of the text that they can write on or a plastic sheet, such as an overhead transparency, to lay over text that cannot be marked on. As students read, ask them to circle difficult or interesting words or phrases and have them mark the end of each sentence in one of three ways:

✓ check mark means they understand this information

! exclamation point indicates that this is new and interesting information

? question mark indicates they do not understand what the sentence means or there is a word that they do not understand.

After reading a specific section of text, the students talk together about how they marked the text. They discuss what information they understand and what was new, and they try to help one another clarify the sections they've marked with question marks.

> Coral reefs are amazing things! The individual coral formations come in all sorts of unusual shapes? Some look like moose antlers or trees! Others resemble cabbages or even giant brains?
>
> Some reefs are huge! Experts say that coral reefs are the largest structures built by any species—even humans! The largest coral reef is the Great Barrier Reef. It stretches for 1,250 miles along the coast of Australia! Some parts of the reef extend 150 miles from the shore! Altogether, the Great Barrier Reef covers 135,000 square miles! That's about the size of the state of New Mexico!

Student-marked codes can quickly show you where students are comprehending or struggling with a text.

ROLL AND ASK (Large or small group)

Provide students with a six-sided cube labeled *Who*, *What*, *Where*, *When*, *Why*, and *How*. After reading a section of text, students take turns rolling the cube and creating a question beginning with the word shown on the cube for the other students to answer. For example, when reading "Goldilocks and the Three Bears," a student may roll *Where* and ask, "Where were the three bears

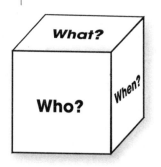

when Goldilocks came to their house?" Creating questions in this way helps students focus on the text, especially when they realize that they have to be able to tell the other students if their answers are correct or not.

Variation 1: Roll the cube once, and ask each student to ask a question starting with that word.

Variation 2: Let each student roll the cube before reading the text and prepare a question while reading, to ask when the text is completed.

QUESTION-ANSWER RELATIONSHIPS (QAR)
(Small or large group, individual)

Many of the questions students ask in Roll and Ask and I Wonder are literal questions, but some require inference and evaluative thinking. Based on the work of Taffy Raphael (1986), QAR teaches students to classify questions into three categories: Right There, Think and Search, and On My Own. Right There questions are literal. The answer is right there in the text, and you can put your finger on it. Think and Search requires more work. The answer is not right there, but you can use information found in the text in several different places, along with some inferring, to answer the question. On My Own questions require prior knowledge on the part of the reader. Once students can identify the types of questions, they can identify the strategies required to answer them.

● When you first teach this activity, combine it with I Wonder and code how you and your students found the answer to a particular question the students posed, either RT (Right There), TS (Think and Search), or OMO (On My Own).

● Give students questions that you've created for the text, along with your answers. Work with students to determine what kinds of questions they are, based on the answers. For example, if my students and I had read "Goldilocks and the Three Bears," I might provide these questions and answers:

1. What did Goldilocks eat? (She ate Baby Bear's porridge.)

2. How did Baby Bear feel when he found his chair? (He was very sad.)

3. Do you think Goldilocks will ever go into someone else's house when no one is home? (I don't think she will.)

● Discuss with students how you found your answers. In the example above, question 1 is *Right There*. My students find that they can put their finger on the answer in the book where it says, "Goldilocks ate Baby Bear's porridge all up." Question 2 is *Think and Search*. The text says Baby Bear began to cry and said, "Someone's broken my chair all to pieces." I infer, "Baby Bear's crying makes me think he was sad, even though the author doesn't say so." Question 3 is *On My Own*. The text doesn't say whether Goldilocks will come back, but she was very frightened when she saw the bears and she jumped out of the window and ran all the way home. I tell students, "I think she probably learned her lesson and won't be going into anyone else's house."

● After students have learned the types of questions, ask them to create Right There, Think and Search, and On My Own questions to ask one another. They may work in small groups or with partners to answer one another's questions, and tell how they found the answers.

● Look at examples of questions found on comprehension assessments to determine the types of questions and the best method to answer them.

GRAPHIC ORGANIZERS (Large or small group, individual)

Graphic organizers are tools to help students think about and organize information from texts they are reading. The forms shown in the chart about informational text on page 157 are useful for collecting and displaying information from expository text and they can also be used with fiction. For example, Venn diagrams (page 189) work well with expository text that compares two or more topics, but they are equally useful for comparing two characters in a story, or two different texts with a similar theme. Sequence charts (page 190) work well to list plot events in order, as well as for describing the steps for making bread. The cause and effect chart (page 191) is equally useful when explaining the causes of precipitation and why the bears left their home. I use the web (page 192) to display main ideas and supporting details and also to describe characters and their traits.

STORY STAR (Large or small group, individual)

The story star (page 193) is another simple organizational tool for reporting the elements of fiction. Students fill in each point of the star with the corresponding information from the text. Younger students can draw as needed. The top point is for recording a connection that students made to the story. The star can be used as a graphic organizer during reading to collect and organize thinking, or afterwards as a summary. It's also useful to have students complete a story star before an oral retelling.

As you teach students to use graphic organizers, it is helpful to have several different forms available so students can select which organizer fits the text or their purpose the best. Some students may find a cause and effect chart useful for thinking about a character, while another student may wish to use the web.

Venn Diagram

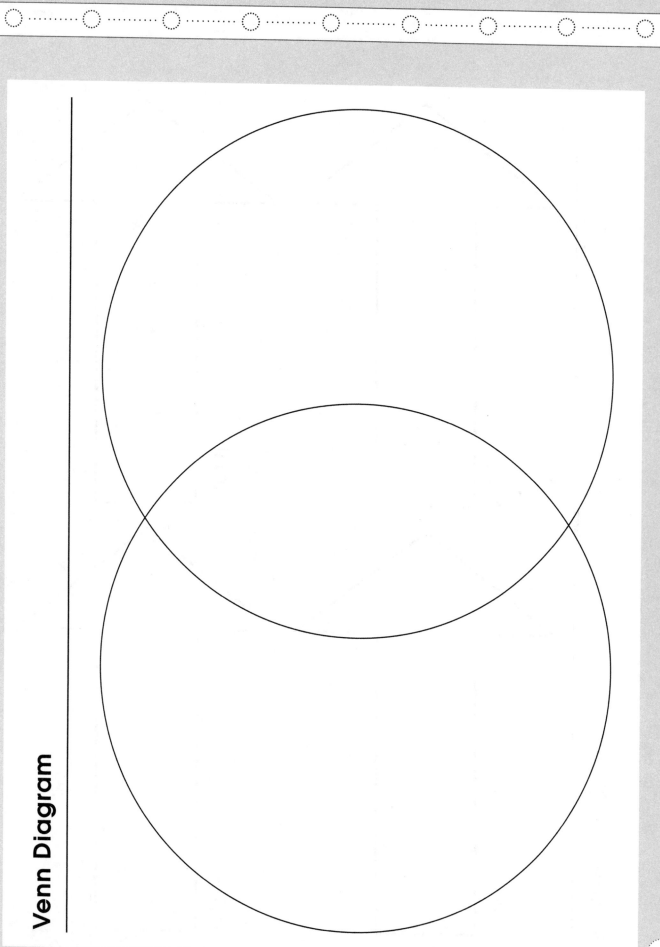

Sequence Chart

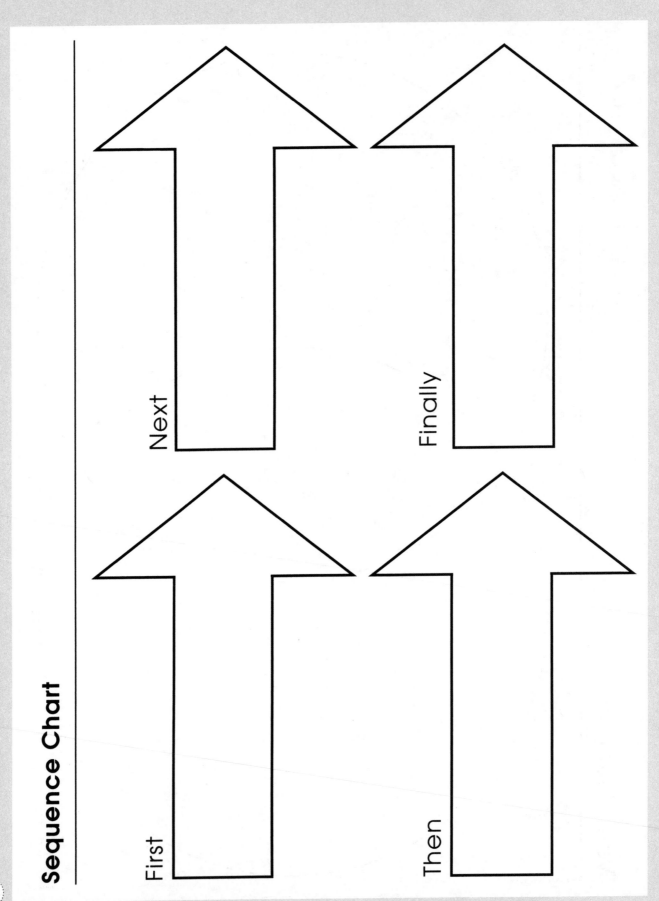

First

Next

Then

Finally

Cause and Effect

Event

Effect

caused →

caused →

caused →

caused →

Web Organizer

Story Star

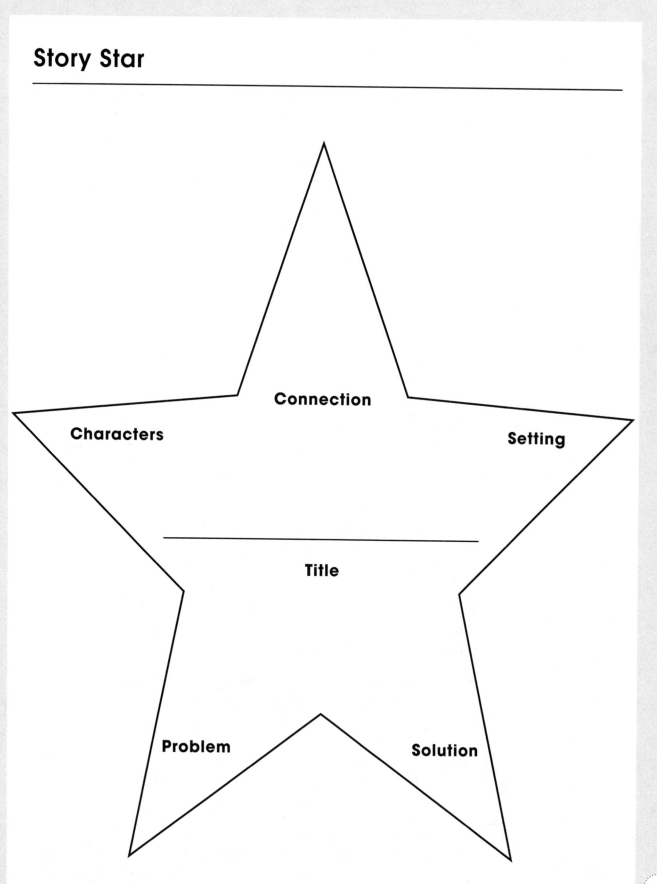

Connection

Characters

Setting

Title

Problem

Solution

RETELLING CARDS FOR FICTION
(Large or small group, individual)

Stories generally have characters, settings, a problem, and events that lead to a resolution. We also hope that students can identify the main idea of the story as well as a theme. For this activity, you need a story with these elements, and prompt cards.

- Make several copies of the reproducible on pages 195–196 in three or four different colors. Select the cards that show elements your students are familiar with. For example, you might give your second graders only the problem, solution, character, and setting cards. Cut out these cards and randomly distribute them for the activity.

- Either read a story aloud or ask students to read a story independently.

- Ask students to identify the part of the story that matches their cards. For example, if you were reading "Goldilocks and the Three Bears" and a student had a "setting: where" card, he or she would listen for the setting and probably identify the three bears' house.

- After reading the text, ask students to get into groups with others who have the same story element card, and discuss what they found. They should come to a consensus.

- Next, students form groups by the colors of their cards. Each story element should be represented in each group. Students then discuss each part of the story, with the person holding the card contributing their element.

Variation for small groups: Make one copy of each story element and pass the cards to individuals or partners. Students identify their elements on their own and then share their findings with the group.

Variation: Let students randomly select cards after the reading is completed. With this variation, they have to listen and be ready to identify all elements of the story.

Retelling Cards

a prediction I made and why

the problem

the solution

description of the main characters

setting: where

setting: when

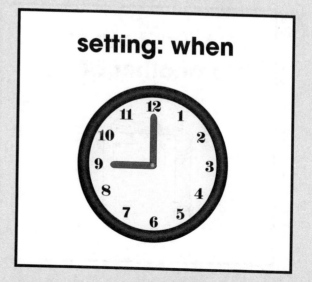

Retelling Cards

the main idea

important plot details

an inference I made

a link I made to my life

a link I made to another book

a link I made to the world

SOMEWHERE, SOMETIME, SOMEBODY RETELL
(Large or small group, individual)

After reading a work of fiction, ask students to select a character from the story and use the Retelling Form (page 198) as a way to organize the elements of the story. I particularly like this activity, since students can select different characters and tell the story from different points of view. If, for example, the "somebody" is Baby Bear, he wants his porridge to cool, which is quite different from what Goldilocks wants. This form works for just about any text that has a problem, and is easy to use for a broad range of grade levels, beginning as early as kindergarten with some simplification.

DRAW AND TELL (Individual)

This activity is especially good for younger students. It is a good introduction to story structure. Ask students to make sketches on the Draw and Tell form (page 199), showing who was in the story, where it happened, something that happened, and how the story ended. After drawing, students write words or sentences to explain their drawings.

STOP AND TALK/WRITE
(Large or small group, individual)

During a read-aloud, shared reading, or a guided reading lesson, stop periodically and ask students to work in pairs to "say something" about the text to their partners. You can designate what you would like them to discuss, for example, "Tell your neighbor what you think the big idea in this section was all about," or "Share a connection you've made." You can also let them tell whatever they are thinking about as they read or listen to the text. At designated points in a text, ask students to stop and write in their reading journals or on sticky notes.

RECIPROCAL TEACHING (Large or small group)

Reciprocal Teaching is an instructional activity originally developed by Annemarie Palinscar (1986) that includes the use of four different comprehension strategies—predicting, questioning, monitoring/clarifying, and summarizing—in tandem. Its effectiveness has been confirmed in the research of the National Reading Panel (p.4-46).

Retelling Form

Name _____ Date _____

Title _____

Somewhere _____

Sometime _____

Somebody _____

Wanted _____

_____

But _____

_____

Then _____

_____

_____

So _____

_____

_____

Finally _____

_____

_____

Next time _____

_____

_____

Draw and Tell

Draw: Who	Draw: Where
Tell	**Tell**
Draw: What happened	Draw: How it ended
Tell	**Tell**

To use Reciprocal Teaching, make four cards for each group of students using the card template on page 201. Students use these cards to work in a group to develop understanding of a text.

- Card 1 is for the Predictor. It says, "Predict. Use clues from the text or illustrations to predict what will happen next or what the text will be about. Say *I think . . . because. . . .*"

- Card 2 is for the Questioner. It says, "Question. Ask questions that have answers in the text. Ask some Think and Search questions, too." Use the question words *who, what, where, when, why, how,* and *what if.*

- Card 3 is for the Clarifier. It says, "Clarify. Look for difficult or confusing words or ideas in the text. Tell how you figured them out. Use the parts of the word that you know. Think about where you've seen that word before. Reread or read on. Look for clues in the text and think about what you know about this topic."

- Card 4 is for the Summarizer. It says, "Summarize. Use your own words to tell the main ideas from the text in order. Use the words *first, next, then,* and *finally* to help you put events in order."

First the group agrees on how much of a text to read. Then they read the section, and use the four cards to respond. In some cases, students rotate tasks, so that each time they stop, they try a different strategy. In other instances, one student takes the role of leader, and at each meeting asks every student to make a prediction, clarify difficult words or ideas, summarize, or ask the group a question.

Reciprocal Teaching works especially well for struggling older readers, in small groups. The procedures can also be used well with younger students if introduced and practiced as part of a whole group lesson before they are asked to use the strategies more independently.

LANGUAGE EXPERIENCE (Large or small group, individual)

For your most struggling students, create and write a text together through shared writing or dictation. Then students can use the text for reading. This language experience approach, made popular by Roach Van Allen and Sylvia Ashton Warner in the 1970s, often has students writing about a shared experience, such as a field trip or science activity, but it is not always necessary. You and your students can create a text about

Reciprocal Teaching Cards

Predict

Use clues from the text or illustrations to predict what will happen next or what the text will be about.

 Hint:
Say, *I think . . . because . . .*

Question

Ask questions that have answers in the text. Ask some Think and Search questions, too.

 Hint:
Use the question words *who, what, where, when, why, how,* and *what if.*

Clarify

Look for difficult or confusing words or ideas in the text. Tell how you figured them out.

Hint: Use the parts of the word that you know. Think about where you've seen that word before. Reread or read on. Look for clues in the text and think about what you know about this topic.

Summarize

Use your own words to tell the main ideas from the text in order.

 Hint:
Use the words *first. next, then,* and *finally* to help you put events in order.

anything—a classroom pet, an upcoming holiday, the seasons, or a book they've read together. A text from a second-grade class appears on page 202.

● Before you start writing, talk with students about the subject.

● Work with students to create the text. In shared writing, the students and teacher "share the pen," with everyone taking turns writing. In true language experience, the teacher does all the writing while the students dictate. The resulting text then becomes the students' reading material.

● You can type it into a book format, and invite students to illustrate each page, similar to the Sketch It strategy described on page 183, or write it onto a large chart.

● You can also use the text as a basis for practicing reading strategies, such as summarizing and asking questions. Language experience is especially effective with students who have meager background knowledge about "book" topics or language. Students who are learning English also benefit from this approach, since the words in the text are from their speaking vocabulary and contain familiar language patterns.

Language Experience Story (Second-Grade Example)

Our Ducks

Our class got six duck eggs. We put them into the incubator. After a few days the eggs started to move around a little bit and get cracks. First we could see some little beaks come poking out of the shells. Then there were some little heads. When the ducks came out they were all wet and tired. They just laid there for a long time. Then they started to quack and move around. Now we have six little ducks in our room. They make lots of noise when we go over to their tub.

One of our ducks was naughty. He kept pecking the other ducks. We put him in time-out in the kindergarten room. When he came back he wasn't naughty anymore. Now they all get along together.

Final Thoughts

There are a broad range of instructional activities and approaches that support comprehension in your classroom. The important thing is that we teach students how to comprehend. It's tempting to use the activities explained above simply as follow-up activities after students read. Remember that these are tools for encouraging students to use comprehension strategies to actively read and understand text. The activities are most effective when introduced as part of the instructional model for comprehension strategies outlined in this chapter. Modeling the strategy and providing guided and scaffolded practice before you expect students to use the activities independently will contribute to their success as readers who "listen to themselves" as they read and comprehend.

Resources and Further Reading

Allington, R. L. (2006). *What really matters for struggling readers* (2nd ed.). Boston: Pearson.

Applegate, M. D., Quinn, K. B., & Applegate, A. J. (2002). Levels of thinking required by comprehension questions in informal reading inventories. *The Reading Teacher, 56*, 174–180.

Beaver, J. & Carter, M. (2006). *Developmental reading assessment* (2nd ed.). Parsippany, NJ: Celebration Press.

Dowhower, S. L. (1999). Supporting a strategic stance in the classroom: A comprehension framework for helping teachers help students to be strategic. *The Reading Teacher, 52*, 672–688.

Duke, N. & Pearson, P. D. (2002). Effective practices for developing reading comprehension. In A. Farstrup and S. Jay Samuels (Eds.), *What research has to say about reading instruction*. Newark, DE: International Reading Association.

Fountas, I. C. and Pinnell, G. (2007). *Fountas & Pinnell benchmark assessment system*. Portsmouth, NH: Heinemann.

Keene, E. O. & Zimmermann, S. (1997). *Mosaic of thought*. Portsmouth, NH: Heinemann.

National Reading Panel. (2000). *Report of the National Reading Panel: Teaching children to read. Report of the subgroups*. Washington, DC: U.S. Department of Health and Human Services, National Institutes of Health.

Oczkus, L. D. (2004). *Reciprocal teaching at work: Strategies for improving reading comprehension*. Newark, DE: International Reading Association.

Palinscar, A. S. & Brown, A. L. (1986). Interactive teaching to promote independent learning from text. *The Reading Teacher, 39*, 771–777.

Raphael, T. E. (1986). Teaching question-answer relationships, revisited. *The Reading Teacher, 39*, 516–523.

Finally

Throughout this book I've given you ways to assess what your students are able to do in reading. For ease of organization, I've divided it into the separate areas of phonemic awareness and phonics, vocabulary, fluency, and comprehension. As you remember from the first chapter, readers use all of these areas in a sophisticated interplay when they read and get the meaning of text. Reading is a dynamic process, and the tool that served a child well in getting the meaning of one text will not necessarily be the best tool for another text, nor will the tool that worked for one child necessarily be the best tool for another child reading the same text.

Remember to notice what your students can do well, not only what needs improvement, and build on their strengths. Effective reading instruction solidifies the skills students currently have and teaches them to do something they can't yet do. I hope the assessments and lesson ideas in this book help you plan what to do next.

Index